LIVE THE LIZZO WAY

NATTY KASAMBALA

LIVE THE LIZZO WAY

100% THAT BOOK YOU NEED

HarperCollins*Publishers*

HarperCollins*Publishers*
1 London Bridge Street
London SE1 9GF

www.harpercollins.co.uk

HarperCollins*Publishers*
Macken House, 39/40 Mayor Street Upper,
Dublin 1, D01 C9W8, Ireland

First published by HarperCollins*Publishers* 2021

10 9 8 7 6 5 4 3 2 1

© HarperCollins*Publishers* 2021

Natty Kasambala asserts the moral right to be identified as the author of this work
Illustrations by Amelia Deacon

A catalogue record of this book is available from the British Library

ISBN 978-0-00-851072-5

Printed and bound by PNB, Latvia

This book is produced from independently certified FSC™ paper
to ensure responsible forest management.

For more information visit: www.harpercollins.co.uk/green

CONTENTS

INTRODUCTION: INSPIRED BY LIZZO

It's safe to say that over the last few years it has been nearly impossible to walk through life without hearing about Lizzo: on your TV, at festivals, on the radio – she has been pretty much everywhere.

If you're ever in doubt when out in the wild, here are some of the tell-tale signs that you're listening to a Lizzo song: playful, punchy lyrics that are instantly convertible into Instagram captions; an anthemic sing-along chorus; the distinct feeling of being able to conquer the world both during and after the song has played out in full.

From topping the charts with her sleeper hit 'Truth Hurts', to sweeping the 2019 Grammys (she was nominated for eight and took home three), to being named *TIME* magazine's Entertainer of the Year 2019, in many ways, it has been Lizzo's 'year' for about three years – and counting.

But, despite popular belief, she's been around for longer than you might think. Since 2014 Lizzo, born Melissa Viviane Jefferson, has been hustling and struggling, honing her craft and finding her sound. She toured endlessly, performed for free and at one point even slept in her car for a year while trying to make it in the biz. Born in Detroit, Michigan, before relocating to Houston, Texas, as a young girl, she dreamed of and was surrounded by music for many years. Influenced by the rich rap culture of Texas, she started rapping with her friends and landed on the stage name 'Lizzo' at the age of just 14.

While at school and the University of Houston, she was classically trained as a flautist, though she soon realised that trying to balance her rap and flute careers at the same time would be unsustainable. In 2013, Lizzo worked to release her first rap album, *Lizzobangers*, which was distinctly hip-hop in sound and was eventually rereleased by a major label. Off the back of this, she was approached by one of her idols – Prince – and subsequently featured on his 2014 album *Plectrumelectrum*, before dropping her second album, *Big GRRRL Small World*, in 2015, which was met by a respectable media response but made no significant cultural waves. It was what came next that signalled the beginning of Lizzo as we know and love her today.

With the release of her 2016 EP *Coconut Oil*, which acted as a reintroduction, the lead single 'Good as Hell' – an exultant, gospel-inspired, feel-good tune – established her as a symbol of self-love, healing and complete positivity. She used the momentum of this to go out and tour the world, converting audiences to the church of Lizzo. From playing supporting slots for HAIM and Florence + the Machine, to guest-judging on *RuPaul's Drag Race*, to soundtracking the 2016 *Barbershop: The Next Cut* feature film, Lizzo's reach became broader than ever before. And she has been grafting ever since.

Thanks to the viral clips of her 'ho and flute' endeavours (her flute now has its own Instagram account and fits seamlessly into her pop identity) and her elaborately theatrical visuals, hilarious personality pieces, countless raunchy Instagram posts and record-breaking hits, Lizzo has morphed into the newest pop phenom. Her single 'Truth Hurts' powered to the top of the Billboard charts three years after its original release, confirming her self-proclamation in the track that she is in fact 'that b*tch', whether people realise it or not.

With every appearance, her infectiously bold presence wins over crowds and bolsters the inspiring message of her music. She's a living example of how you can become your most authentic self and be comfortable in your own skin, having graced the covers of *Rolling Stone*, *Vogue*, *Elle*, *Billboard*, *NME* and so many more sporting daring fashion choices, audacious hairstyles and her signature self-confidence. On stage, she's backed up by all plus-size dancers and routinely transitions into freestyle flute interludes, often with a twerk as the final flourish. Unafraid to have fun, break the mould and be vulnerable, Lizzo is also candid about her own struggles and has become an advocate for body positivity, the importance of looking after your mental health and relationships, and more.

And she's clear about who she does it for, too. As well as crediting her career to those who have come before her – Aretha Franklin and Missy Elliott being two of her biggest inspirations – Lizzo dedicates her music to those for whom she can be a source of inspiration and representation. And with a rabid fandom dubbed the 'lizzbians', her own sub-genre of memes and celebrity co-signs from the likes of Harry Styles, Rihanna and the cast of Netflix's *Queer Eye*, it's clear that the world is ready to receive her. She defies all the prescribed rules of how a popstar is meant to act, look and feel about themselves, and for that reason, she has become a beacon of hope for the marginalised as well as the mainstream.

The release of her third studio album in 2019, *Cuz I Love You*, only solidified her stardom. With its iconic intimate nude portrait on the cover and the string of powerhouse ballads that showcase her chops as a singer as much as a rapper, the record confirmed all suspicions that Lizzo was ushering in a new era of pop – one that gives you permission to be physically and emotionally naked, to reject toxic beauty standards and cultural norms and to claim back concepts of self-love in a meaningful, unabashed way. 'Soulmate' declares her as her own destined 'other half', 'Jerome' rids her of a toxic relationship and 'Like a Girl' sees her dispel female stereotypes to reclaim the misogynistic cliché as an expression of power, femininity and strength. In a world that can feel judgemental and prescriptive, Lizzo shows us how to be inclusive, liberated and unapologetic in the way we live our lives.

This book is a celebration of the joy-filled movement she has helped create, exploring the lessons we can take from her music, career and wider approach to life. Guided by Lizzo's empowering example, it will arm you with the tips, tricks and wisdom to be fearless and loving, and to feel beautiful inside and out.

6 When I have to make decisions, I always choose honesty and I always stay true to myself, because I know at the end of the day that is what's going to remain. 9

'That time you called me talented? Put "multi" in front of it.'

LIZZO'S

LESSONS IN SELF-CONFIDENCE

Though Lizzo's rise to fame might seem like an overnight success, it really wasn't. In reality, she had been working for almost 10 years by the time fame found her, and although she may have felt lost, confused or impatient at times during her journey to get where she is today, in the end, believing in herself and her talent paid off. Her path has been one of risk-taking, knock-backs and self-doubt, but ultimately it's clear that self-confidence came out on top and is now knitted into every fibre of her being, from the music she makes to how she performs it live.

LET'S START AT THE BEGINNING

There is clearly something in the Texan water for the place to have nurtured so many of the biggest artists in the world today, from Beyoncé and Solange to Normani (formerly of girl group Fifth Harmony) and Megan Thee Stallion. As one of the main hubs of Southern rap and hip-hop, particularly in the 1990s and early 2000s, Texas was naturally the place where Melissa began to dip her toes into the world of MCs and lyrical wordplay. At the age of 14, she even formed a musical group at school with her friends, adorably named the Cornrow Clique, who used to freestyle rap in the cafeteria during lunch. This was also the genesis of the name 'Lizzo' – inspired by a mix of her own name shortened to 'Lissa' and Jay-Z's 2004 hit single 'Izzo (H.O.V.A)'.

As well as beginning this journey of hip-hop discovery, Lizzo was also flexing her classical muscles. When she was 12 years old, she was picked by her music teacher to start learning the flute. Long story short, she was a natural. Lizzo remembers this period as a time when she felt she was living

FUN FACT

Learning how to play an instrument is a super-rewarding hobby. Though it can feel pretty daunting, there are so many reported benefits to it. Here are a couple of reasons why you might want to consider heading down to your local music shop.

GOOD FOR THE BRAIN

Musical training has been shown to improve long-term memory and brain development if picked up at a young age. It gives you really great experience in processing and retaining information, as well as honing your decision-making and reflexes.

MULTITASKING

Playing music can have a really great impact on your multisensory skills – aka: your ability to process multiple things happening at the same time. Learning an instrument is a demanding activity that combines a number of senses all at once. You are using your vision to read the music, your touch to play the instrument and your hearing to listen, alongside your memory and motor skills to actually comprehend and play the notes.

STRESS-REDUCTION

Listening to and playing music has been found to be extremely beneficial for balancing moods, helping to manage anxiety and boost productivity. Music that you enjoy listening to makes your brain release more happy hormones, such as dopamine, which not only helps your emotional health, but also your general cognitive function.

a double life: 'There was flute Melissa and then there was Lizzo. So I had these two personalities that I was starting to develop.' The decision to play that particular instrument was pretty random, as Lizzo jokes: 'I could have been playing the clarinet and twerking!'

If you have an instrument at home, try setting aside half an hour a day to practise it or teach yourself a few notes if you're a beginner. If you don't have an instrument, don't worry! Belting out a few Lizzo tunes is a fantastic way to boost your mood.

Lizzo got to grips with the flute in record time and even joined the school marching band. To this day she regularly refers to herself as a 'band nerd', having been teased at school for her extracurriculars and enthusiasm to learn. Eventually, after surviving high school – in the way so many of us do, just about – Lizzo graduated in 2006 and was accepted to study classical flute at the University of Houston on a music scholarship.

Lizzo describes her father as being fairly strict when she was young, but only in the sense that if you had a goal, he would push you to achieve it. In her case, that goal was to be the best. She wanted to become an acclaimed classical musician and play in a symphony orchestra. She had been training with the principal flautist from the Houston Ballet since junior year of high school, and she had plans after her degree to go and study at the Paris Conservatory to hone her craft further. And so, she strived for it. She was excelling in class, too, or, in Lizzo's own words, 'smokin' them hoes in the masterclasses'. There was a style and flair to her flute playing that was hard to emulate and it would shine during group performance classes. It was her sturdy self-belief

that allowed Lizzo to put her stamp on classical flute from a young age. And being unafraid of breaking the rules and regulations of genre is something that would continue to serve her for many years to come.

Unfortunately, during her time at university, Lizzo's father's health began to fail. Her motivation for studying the flute then became all about the possibility of earning a living through her playing to support her dad. If she could succeed, she could make enough money to care for him. That was the thinking. But overwhelmed by life on campus, mounting emotional pressures and money worries, in 2010 Lizzo made the decision to drop out of college halfway through her degree. It was one of the hardest things she'd ever done, choosing to give up on her classical dream, and she admits that, for a while, she was ashamed of it, figuring she'd let everyone down.

Not long after, when she was just 21 years old, her father Michael Jefferson passed away, and for a moment Lizzo's world stood still. Her dad had been one of the main driving forces of her learning and success, and now that he had passed, she saw only bleakness. She felt lost and completely without direction, temporarily believing that everything she'd achieved in her life so far had been for nothing. It was one of her lowest points. For some time Lizzo couldn't speak to anyone and instead isolated herself. She left home and made the decision to live out of her car while she pursued her career as a solo artist, which ended up being for about a year. And by 2011, she decided to bet on herself by making the move with a friend to Minneapolis, Minnesota, to chase her rap dreams in the burgeoning music scene of this new city.

> **❝ To be embraced by Prince and co-signed, I am eternally grateful for that. ❞**

Self-confidence isn't something that always comes naturally to people; it's something you usually have to work towards. You're probably familiar with the phrase 'fake it till you make it', but at the same time, it's also best for us to be honest and transparent about our doubts and fears in order to overcome them. And that's what Lizzo has done time and time again. Though she made the leap to commit herself to her career as a commercial artist instead of a classical musician, she wasn't instantly filled with infinite self-belief in her own talents and ability. Performing in a number of groups over the next few years, Lizzo gained experience as a songwriter and performer that straddled polar-opposite genres and sounds, while easing into the industry bit by bit. Electro-pop duo Lizzo and the Larva Ink was one of the first iterations, followed by three-piece rap and R&B group The Chalice, made up of all women – her best friend and tour DJ Sophia Eris and Claire De Lune. The collective released their debut project *We Are The Chalice* in 2012, to a decent local reception. A year later, 2013 saw the release of Lizzo's first solo project, an energetic rap album entitled *Lizzobangers*, which gained her a lot of media attention: a positive review in the *Guardian*, a few support slots and eventually a re-release by Virgin Records. Meanwhile, The Chalice were having their own wins.

One of the reasons Minneapolis is famed is as the hometown of the late, inimitable, Prince. And in 2014 he was mentoring and supporting a number of promising young black female musicians. After a solid year or so of grinding hard at music, doing shows across the state (some of which Lizzo remembers as being literally empty except for her own mother, who would come to support her), Lizzo and her bandmates were selected to be taken under Prince's wing. They would visit his studio regularly, although sometimes only communicating with him through speakers in the wall. The group even went on to feature on a track called 'Boytrouble' from Prince's album *Plectrumelectrum*, and Lizzo still brands the time she spent in his home and compound Paisley Park as 'a fairytale'.

While that period gave her invaluable music-industry experience ahead of her signing to Atlantic Records at the end of 2015, Lizzo also reflects that part of the attraction of being in a group was that she didn't feel all that confident about stepping into the spotlight on her own. In an interview with radio show *The Breakfast Club* she admitted, 'I was nervous to be out front and centre by myself. I felt that because I looked the way that I looked that people didn't really wanna look at just me … I was like, nobody wants to hear what I have to say.' Nowadays, it's hard to believe that was ever the case.

GOING SOLO

What Lizzo did always have in those moments, however, was an unshakeable belief that when the time was right, her path would become clear and she would know her purpose. 'I told God, I said, if I'm meant to be a solo artist, you are going to make it easy for me and it's just going to flow and be natural.' Sometimes self-confidence is as simple as visualising what you want, believing that it will happen to you and trusting that everything will make sense in the end.

The first step towards achieving your goals is knowing what they are. It sounds obvious, but it can actually be harder than it seems to break down and name exactly what your aims are in life, at work and in the relationships you care about.

❝ This is the time I was born in and this is the mission I was given and I'm so blessed that I can turn my emotions and my struggles into self-care through music. ❞

Sometimes it's a case of working backwards: figuring out what your ultimate goal is and then deciphering the best possible steps towards that end. Doing so explicitly and regularly is a great way to stay motivated and hold yourself accountable. Use the space below to figure out what you would really like to achieve. Draw a picture if that's easier. While you're considering this question, try to dispense with any negative thoughts and fears that might be clouding your judgement or dampening your ambition. Be as specific, honest and bold as possible.

Eventually, Lizzo stumbled on her very own superpower. In 2014, she agreed to film an interview for YouTube platform StyleLikeU as part of their 'What's Underneath' series, in which the interviewee is asked to answer questions about their life and philosophies, while removing items of clothing in front of a camera – the idea being that by the end of the interview, the subject is naked both emotionally and physically. In her episode, Lizzo was asked the following question: what do you love the most about your body? She responds with a sheepish smile and admits that she had recently been asked this in a therapy session and hadn't been able to give an answer. 'I kept naming things about my personality.' She goes on to tell a story about how she recently fell off a cliff and was left with scrapes all over her arms and body. 'It made me appreciate my skin' – and as she says this, her voice breaks and she starts to cry – 'and this is something I was born with. You can't buy this at the store.'

Looking back at that moment in an interview with Jameela Jamil on the I Weigh YouTube channel, Lizzo acknowledged that the revelation was transformative for her as both a person and an artist: 'I was like, I've never realised that before! I never could put into words anything about my body that I loved and I didn't realise how much I loved my skin. But also my skin is the thing that's most weaponised and used against me and the thing that marginalises me and I was like, wow … and then I wrote a song about it.'

The song she went on to write was aptly called 'My Skin' and features a snippet from the original interview. In it, Lizzo sings softly about the power and weight that her brown skin holds in this world, its permanence and its beauty. It marks the beginning of the Lizzo we know today, stepping into her strengths as an uplifting voice for first herself and, as a result, for so many underdogs globally. 'My Skin' connected with so many people, it made Lizzo realise that turning her emotions into music that could help others was the right mission for her.

Still, it's been a long journey from that day to this. Only after finding something beautiful within herself did Lizzo

6 The first concert I ever attended was my own imaginary concert in my head: I was the headliner and I was the opening act and I was the DJ and the back-up singers. 9

discover not only inspiration for a song lyric, but a purpose in life: to spread that message of self-love and empowerment to others and speak it into existence for herself, too. Lizzo has said that being herself was the biggest creative risk she ever took, 'but it 100 per cent paid off'. And though it sounds straightforward, in a world that hasn't always represented our diverse society fairly, the impact of Lizzo being herself, and being received on a global scale in the way that she has been, cannot be understated.

'I went through a long process of learning to love myself. And it started with wanting to be somebody else and actually not loving myself.' A lot of the time, when you feel doubtful or insecure, witnessing those who are confident and daring can feel beyond intimidating, as though it's a place you can't quite imagine ever reaching. But it's so important to know and believe that the shakiness you might

❝ Always push yourself and believe in the magic you're creating. ❞

be feeling in yourself now is not only natural, but also an essential part of your own journey towards knowing your worth. Without it, it can't really be called growth, can it? And where's the fun in that?

Sadly, we can't hit fast-forward on the difficult bits. Lizzo knows there's no easy fix. Instead, it's about making a reasonable, pragmatic choice based on the simple facts of life. 'One day I was like, yo, I'm gonna be in this body forever ... you either live your life not liking her or you live your life trying to love her ... ever since then I've been working on loving myself, and now I'm getting married to myself!' Here, of course, she's referring to her self-love-struck music video for her chart-topping hit 'Truth Hurts'. Sitting at over 235 million views at the time of writing, the short visual sees her lace-clad and veiled-up for an intimate marriage ceremony, in which it's revealed at the end that she is getting hitched to herself. It's a cheeky, direct reflection of the message she continues to preach consistently in tracks like 'Juice' and 'Soulmate': that once you believe in your own sauce wholeheartedly, the rest is just a bonus.

LIZZO'S IDOLS

Alongside everyone's favourite icon, Beyoncé, who Lizzo routinely cites as a direct influence, urging her to work harder and be better in everything she does, Lizzo was also inspired by the careers of rapper, actor and producer Queen Latifah, as well as rap veteran Missy Elliott. In them, she began to see from a young age the possibilities of a flourishing career for herself and it spurred on her passion further. Born in Portsmouth, Virginia, Elliott became not just a hip-hop staple but part of the vanguard in the 1990s,

collaborating with childhood friend and producer Timbaland first as part of songwriting/producing collective Swing Mob before launching her own solo career in 1997 to critical acclaim. Lizzo raves about Missy Elliott whenever she gets the chance: 'Not only being a writer, a producer, performer and a style icon, but she was winning Grammys and she was at the top of the charts. And for me, that gave me the belief in myself.' In an interview with *Vogue* magazine, Lizzo describes both Latifah and Elliott as 'women who looked like me and who were successful in the ways I wanted to be successful'. By that, she means a combination of things: they were black, they were women, they were extremely confident and charismatic, and lastly, their bodies did not necessarily conform to mainstream standards of beauty at that time and were never the direct focus of their careers. Any of that sounding familiar?

Things came full circle for Lizzo when none other than the great Missy Elliott ended up featuring on her twerk-happy single 'Tempo' from her own Grammy Award-winning studio album *Cuz I Love You*. It was a moment that had been years in the making and yet was still utterly surreal to the singer: she had gone from being a 'weird black girl' watching her in music videos to collaborating with her as a peer. Missy herself had the following glowing words to say of Miss Melissa: 'She shows the world what strength and perseverance look like,' adding that she was 'empowering, liberating and fun … with a side order of ratchet sauce'.

THE BEAUTY OF LIZZO

So we've covered Lizzo's journey to her own self-acceptance and the people who helped bring that to the surface. The last piece of the puzzle is how that translates into her becoming that same kind of inspiration for others. Because only in knowing her own worth and believing in her talent is she able to radiate a confidence that uplifts those around her, through her songs, on her social media or at her iconic live performances.

After the epiphany Lizzo had with her single 'My Skin', it was on her 2016 EP *Coconut Oil* that she was fully able to realise her vision, creating a body of work dedicated to healing and celebration, with a specific focus on people like her: black women. Even the title is a nod to the natural ingredient used by black women to care for and pamper their hair, skin and bodies. It was a clear statement of Lizzo's identity, which helped one specific group of her ever-growing fanbase to feel seen and heard in a way that they often aren't by popular culture.

Her three-time Grammy Award-winning third studio album *Cuz I Love You* broadened that reach even further but held the same aim at its core: to spread happiness and positivity on a grand scale. The way in which she sings throughout the project with complete freedom, backed by big, bold sounds and lyrics that range from the personal to the inspirational, is enough to make you feel like it's okay to be loud, to experience the full range of emotions and to talk about them. 'Like a Girl' sees her explicitly subvert the trope of what it is to do something 'like a girl' at all. With the phrase commonly used as a way of diminishing someone's effort and to imply that femininity means weakness or even ineptitude, Lizzo compares it instead to running for president, living in total independence and holding both power and beauty firmly in your hands.

She harnesses the same energy during her live shows. Whether it's bringing them in for backing vocals, giving captivating solo flute breaks or leaving them with the mantra 'I love you, you are beautiful and you can do anything', Lizzo always takes the opportunity to shower her audience with positive energy and love, building them up to do the same when they get home.

'It's completely life-changing,' plus-size influencer Gabi Gregg said of seeing Lizzo perform live for the first time. 'When you get to see her, it's so impactful and almost brings tears to your eyes because [you think], I knew that was missing my whole life, but I had no idea how much it would mean to actually see it.' While New Orleans musician and collaborator Big Freedia said, 'Her messages about strength and her body-positive image are having an impact on people everywhere.' Arguably, the most profound part of Lizzo morphing into this universal symbol of hope and strength, loved by millions from all walks of life, is the key message that she makes sure to repeat whenever she can: if you can love her, then you can love yourself.

6 As a black woman, I make music for people from an experience that is from a black woman. I'm making music that hopefully makes other people feel good and helps me discover self-love. **9**

‘ It may come as a surprise to some of y'all that I'm not working out to have your ideal body type, I'm working out to have my ideal body type. And you know what type that is? None of your f***ing business. ’

LIZZO

SAYS LOVE YOUR BODY

One of the biggest talking points around Lizzo when she first entered the public sphere was her appearance. At 5 foot 10 inches tall, this beautiful black woman with an unparalleled wig collection, plus-size frame and a wardrobe full of leotards and bikinis wasn't exactly the blueprint for what popstars typically looked like, until now.

‘I learned to actually look all of my insecurities in the face, call them by their name and fall in love with them. ’

And when you twin all of that combination with her now-unshakeable confidence and charisma, which seeks to flaunt and celebrate bodies like hers, what you end up with is a truly exhilarating role model for the next generation. One who represents those who have often been erased, ignored or – worse – actively rejected by the mainstream media.

Historically, standards of beauty in the arts, from fashion to music to film, have remained narrow and restrictive, focusing on deliberately unattainable goals while telling you to strive for them anyway. When Lizzo arrived on the scene to shake things up it was truly timely and necessary, but many people had a lot of catching up to do. Lizzo's efforts to break down the stigmas and proscriptions about what certain body shapes can wear and do didn't come without backlash. She explains: 'In 2014, when I was wearing a leotard on stage and saying I love myself, with two big girls also in leotards, I think people were like, how dare she? How dare she love herself? How could she?'

YOUR BODY IS NONE OF THEIR BUSINESS

There was this peculiar mix of outrage and straight-up bafflement at the fact that this woman was big, loud and dressing for herself instead of others on such a global stage. There she was, wearing the sorts of outfits and expressing the kind of confidence that had previously been reserved for those within a very narrow size range. And the fatphobia jumped straight out of people. For everyone from internet trolls to public figures, Lizzo's body was free fodder for debate and abuse.

The most insidious part of fatphobic language is that it's often seen as more acceptable than fat people themselves are in society. With weight-loss programmes like *The Biggest Loser* and *The Big Fat Truth* helping to stigmatise bigger bodies over the years, fatness has become not just an issue of health, but also morality. In short, being fat equals 'bad', 'shame', 'punishment', while not being fat equals 'good', 'right', 'reward'. For all these reasons and more, when fitness trainer Jillian Michaels disagreed with the widespread celebration of Lizzo, she took it upon herself

FUN FACT

Lizzo was teased for her shoes in middle school. She recalls how her wider-than-average feet would make her shoes slope off to the side as a kid, and other children would make fun of her for having weird shoes. The silver lining, which she shouted out after her chat with David Letterman, is, 'Now I have custom shoes so, HA! Make fun of me now!'

to condemn it publicly. In January 2020, during an interview for Buzzfeed News, the celebrity PT questioned why exactly Lizzo's body was being celebrated. She went on to add that although she loves her music, 'it isn't going to be awesome if she gets diabetes'.

A lot of the time, critiques about the body-positivity movement claim to come from genuine concerns about obesity rates or the general health and wellbeing of plus-sized people. However, these knee-jerk reactions are often founded on double standards.

Yes, there are health risks that increase with obesity and inactive lifestyles, but there are also people with larger bodies who live healthier lifestyles than their skinnier counterparts. After all, there are a ton of extremely unhealthy habits that can pose an increased risk to your health, which aren't visible at all: for example, drinking, smoking and recreational drug use. This is not an argument *for* obesity, but it is an observation that symptoms that present themselves externally, such as weight – regardless of whether you lead an active, healthy lifestyle or not – seem to invite unwarranted and speculative public criticisms, while those who are slim and therefore outwardly healthy-looking are permitted to live their lives freely.

We live in a digital age where unhealthy lifestyles are continuously promoted to us: from record-breaking desserts to calorific diner challenges and wacky viral food trends like burgers covered in layers of gravy and cheese. When food bloggers and platform hosts who fit a more conventional ideal of a healthy body type promote these calorific meals and binge-eating tendencies, they aren't lambasted anywhere near as much as those who merely dare to exist

‘I was politicised because of the things that I wore. Being a big black woman, wearing what I wore on stage was instantly political and it made a statement.’

in larger bodies. Lizzo is someone who visibly lives a very active lifestyle and is more than able to perform for over an hour on stage while landing choreography, live vocals and freestyle flute solos. So if some people ignore the fact that she is clearly very fit because she doesn't conform to their ideal of a 'healthy body', that's not her problem – or yours. Body-shaming tactics not only stigmatise fatness and encourage shame and self-loathing, they also assume that weight is synonymous with health. So until Lizzo's medical records – or anybody else's for that matter – have been posted with an explicit request for public feedback, any concerns for her health appear not only disingenuous, but also extremely invasive.

While Lizzo didn't give a detailed response to Jillian Michaels's comments, she did address the conversations and speculations around her health more generally with a single TikTok video. In June 2020, she posted a compilation video with footage of her working out, posing in lingerie and swimwear, soundtracked by the iconic softly-spoken words: 'Health is not just determined by what you look like on the outside, health is also what happens on the inside and a lot of y'all need to do a f***ing cleanse for your insides. Namaste, have a great day.' And to top it all off, her caption for the video included the send-off: 'If you're watching this, just know you're beautiful!'

Lizzo has talked about how little niggling comments over the years can have a big impact on your perceptions. She uses the example of somebody telling her that she could never have short hair because it 'doesn't look good on big girls'. 'It's like a little mosquito bite. You don't even know it's there. But soon you look up, you're covered in

mosquito bites. And you're like, "Oh my God, I have all of these things." But they were so normalised to me, because they were so innocent.' It takes time and energy to unpack these comments and start the process of relearning.

We all need to adopt a little more of that attitude towards external pressures to look a certain way. We are the only people who fully know ourselves, how we live, how we feel and what we need to be happy (although sometimes that's still a mystery). So, in a nutshell, the opinions of others are completely irrelevant to our lives, especially when those opinions are unprompted and uninformed. It may not be necessary to create viral content showcasing your physical ability to a huge audience, but I do encourage you to try to walk through life with a little more of that carefree attitude. Feel secure in the knowledge that anyone who goes out of their way to make you feel bad about yourself is clearly dealing with their own internal issues, and the best way to prevent yourself from getting caught in their riptide of negativity is to just let their words wash over you.

ACTIVITY

SELF-AFFIRMATION MANTRAS

The word 'mantra' is Sanskrit for the terms 'mind' and 'release'. Finding words or phrases that you can repeat in moments of anxiety or to start your day can be a really great way to ground yourself and shift your outlook in life.

Here is a list of affirming phrases that you can write on Post-it notes and place around your house to remind you in your weaker moments of how beautiful and worthy you are. You could even try writing them all down on small pieces of paper and hiding them in jacket pockets and bags for the future you to find and feel good.

I am love, I am loving, I am loved.

I do not compare myself to others, I love myself for who I am.

I am exactly where I need to be right now.

My strengths are greater than my struggles.

I will let go of what I cannot control.

I am strong and beautiful and worthy of greatness.

My mistakes do not define me, I am doing my best.

My feelings are valid.

I am enough.

I accept and love myself unconditionally.

THE PLUS SIDE

It's good to focus on the bright side! Of course, one of the biggest impacts of Lizzo's meteoric rise is that it has been one of such inclusive celebration and appreciation and, most importantly, the normalisation of diverse body types. It has been less concerned with pleading for acceptance from mainstream gatekeepers and more worried about liberating those who felt pressured to be silent or invisible, or who doubted themselves because of the way they look.

You know that voice that creeps into your head when you're in a shop or browsing online and something super-striking catches your eye? Let's say it's a fluffy hot-pink crop top. You look at it and think to yourself, ooo, that's cute! But before you know it, that little voice inside your head has added, *Yeah, for someone else.* Or maybe it's, *But you couldn't pull it off.* Or, *It's not the right shape for your frame.* Or, *That's waaay too extra.* Well, I'm here to tell you that voice is an idiot (no offence, as technically that voice is still part of your subconscious). You know what happens when you wear something bright and dramatic? The sun still rises and sets, the world keeps turning, time rolls on. The only difference is that you did something you wanted to do. And you have this great new top.

Here in the world of Lizzo, that's what it's all about. Reclaiming the freedom to do what you want, how you want and when you want, as long as it's not causing harm. The world didn't implode because they saw Lizzo, a big black woman, twerking in a leotard while playing the flute on stage and being authentically herself. And the same is true for you.

In Lizzo's cover interview for *Rolling Stone* magazine she credited this same sentiment as the reason why she

stopped caring what people think: 'We eventually get used to everything ... So people just gon' have to get used to my ass.' She's right. At the end of the day, it's your life for the living. Everyone else just has to get used to it.

‘ My first celebrity crush was me. ’

MIRROR, MIRROR

In the same way that Lizzo spreads positivity to promote self-belief, she also uses her platform to actively showcase beautiful people in all shapes and sizes. From her back-up dancers on tour to her music video castings, she's creating a complete world that sees the beauty and strength in everybody. During her performance for NPR's Tiny Desk Concert, she preached in her outro: 'If you can love my big black ass at this tiny-ass desk, you can love yourself.'

Lizzo takes the adoration she gets from her fans and holds it up as a mirror to themselves. If we showed ourselves the same amount of love as we do our idols, the world would be a far happier place. And knowing that it's love you clearly already have to give should make that journey to self-love a little easier. Because who could deserve it more than the person you spend all day every day with?

And that's what Lizzo's music is all about: making sure that no matter what other people think of you, you are more than aware of your value and are definitely not asking their permission to live your truth. Back-to-back on her most recent album *Cuz I Love You*, the tracks 'Juice' and 'Soulmate' both contain unashamed lyrics about falling in love with the woman in the mirror. 'Lingerie' is a sultry ode to (you guessed it!) lounging around in lingerie and

ACTIVITY

YOUR BODY IS YOUR TEMPLE

One of the things that empowered Lizzo to learn to love and celebrate her own body was just the fact that, no matter what happens in life, your body will be yours forever. And it does so many incredible things, goes through so much and bounces back even when you least expect it. It is the thing that nourishes you, houses all your thoughts and feelings, communicates with and connects you to others.

With all that in mind, write down your five favourite parts of your body. They can be big or small or things that only you know about. Maybe it's your particularly long eyelashes or the way your hair forms perfect little springy coils. It could be your button nose or your strong arms, the colour of your eyes or that random beauty mark on the top of your foot. Really take time to study yourself and get familiar with your body.

In those moments when you might find yourself comparing what you have to what others have, remind yourself that without being born into this exact collection of cells and atoms, you wouldn't be who you are today – you might not even be sitting here reading this book! And that this bag of bones is going to be with you for the long haul, so treat it like you would a friend – with patience, love and respect.

1 ....

2 ....

3 ....

4 ....

5 ....

ode to (you guessed it!) lounging around in lingerie and 'Tempo' is a song for the thick girls to break it down to. Her defiant spirit even trickles down to the cover artwork, with a stunning naked portrait of Lizzo that feels both daring and incredibly intimate. A declaration that even when stripped of all the extravagance, politics and showmanship, she's still a work of art.

DIVERSIFYING THE MOVEMENT

Lizzo is also not afraid to call out the body-positivity movement when it strays from its own aims. With the new enthusiasm for body-positivity as more of a hashtag than a life philosophy, the movement can be white-washed, beautified and commercialised, forgetting who it is there to serve and liberate. Author of *Fattily Ever After*, Stephanie Yeboah wrote for *Vogue* on where the movement is currently falling short: 'We've gone from seeing the movement be all about plus-size adulation and celebration to it now being centred on "acceptably fat" women: beautiful women with extreme hourglass shapes, typically white or light-skinned, with small waists, big hips and high cheekbones.' In a nutshell, the lack of diversity when it comes to race, body shapes and genders is just enforcing a new – but still restrictive – set of beauty standards onto plus-size bodies, when the whole point of body-positivity should be to abolish rigid standards altogether.

In the fashion industry particularly, concepts of what it is to be plus-size are still pretty archaic. The label extends to

❛ I think my story has been more about refining who I am versus creating it. ❜

❛ I've come to terms with body dysmorphia and evolved. The body-positive movement is doing the same thing. We're growing together, and it's growing pains, but I'm just glad that I'm attached to something so organic and alive. **❜**

6 My message can't change, my message can't be trendy. This is who I am. 9

anyone from a UK size 12 or US size 16 upwards, with the general rule that to be a successful plus-size model you still have to have 'good body proportions'. The ridiculous rule they use to decide this is that generally your waist should still be around 10 inches smaller than your hips. It's the reason why plus-size representation in the mainstream still perpetuates unattainable standards – that the only way to be curvy is to conform to these 'appealing' templates in which you miraculously only gain weight in all the right places.

Now shying away from the umbrella term of 'body positivity' in favour of wanting to normalise her body, Lizzo explains her reasoning: 'I'm glad that this conversation is being included in the mainstream narrative. What I don't like is how the people that this term was created for are not benefitting from it. Girls with back fat, girls with bellies that hang, girls with thighs that aren't separated, that overlap. Girls with stretch marks. You know, girls who are in the 18-plus club.' In short, Lizzo's concern is that as body positivity has extended further into the mainstream, it has moved away from its goals and has actually begun to replicate the same erasure that it was created to fight against. It's simply failing to show the full picture.

And she makes sure to remind people that the movement's roots are in true inclusivity. As fashionable as it might be at the moment, it's important to focus on the fact that once it's no longer en vogue, there will still be big, beautiful people who live and breathe it. That's why Lizzo is

6 All of the ways that I felt excluded are the ways that I'm helping people feel included. Because if you just open your eyes and see, everybody's going through the same s***. It's the same struggle. We're just different colours and different sizes. **9**

in it for the long haul. 'I realise that right now somehow my messes have happened to hit an apex with culture and it's just synced up. But I also know that even when that moment has passed I have to continue to talk about this.' The people who the body-positivity movement was created by and for will still need it 10, 20, 30 years down the line – for them, it's not a phase.

For all those who think they can't join in with the body-positivity movement because they're not quite comfortable posing in bathing suits yet or don't look like the models on the billboards, please know that those bodies in the ads and on TV aren't accurate representations of the sheer diversity of body shapes out there either. The only body you need to be paying attention to and learning to love is the one you see when you look in the mirror. That's the one to focus on, nurture, embrace and care for, because in some form or other, it'll be with you forever.

WHERE DO WE GO FROM HERE?

Not only does Lizzo want to diversify the body-positivity movement, she also wants to push the conversations around it further into the future. As a society, we should be doing more than just shouting loud and proud about diverse body types in an attempt to drown out the choruses of disapproval. At this stage, that's the bare minimum. Instead, the goal should be to reach a point where body diversity is completely normalised: not a courageous act of revolution, but simply a fact of life, like any physical trait.

Lizzo has made clear her stance as an icon of and activist for body positivity: 'I'm sick of being an activist just because I'm fat and black, I wanna be an activist because

‘They thought they were complimenting me by saying that I was unapologetic. I was like, what do I have to apologise for?’ I'm intelligent, because I care about issues, because my music is good, because I wanna help the world.' Diverse body shapes will only be truly normalised when we reach the point where their existence is not a topic of debate. It will be a time when big women can get on with their lives without being called 'brave' for doing exactly the same thing as skinny women who are simply called 'beautiful'. Excessive praise of a body-confident plus-size woman can have a harmful subtext. The term 'brave' implies she has something to be scared of, that she is fighting a battle that should make her want to hide in a dark corner. Brave is fighting a fire or saving a drowning child. It shouldn't take an act of immense courage and fortitude for a fat woman to love herself or like how she looks in a picture. It shouldn't have to happen against all the odds. Until we reach a point where plus-size celebration is no longer a newsworthy story of resistance and political statements, we will still be living in a society where people of these body shapes are having to fight just to survive and thrive.

So next time your chubby friend posts that bikini pic and your fingers are hovering over the keyboard searching for 'b', 'r' and 'a' or the clapping-hands emoji as if she's just run a marathon, instead type 'beautiful' or 'stunning' or 'flames emoji x10' like you would for any of your slimmer friends, and then go about your day. That's how we normalise.

❝ Hopefully by existing, there can just be more opportunities for people that look like me that are, you know, beyond what a trend is. And that they're there on the merit of their talent. They're there on the merit of their beauty. And they're there because they're good enough. **❞**

‘That's how hit records are made! They're made from the heart. They're made from tears, they're made from fears, and they're made from happy endings.’

One of the hardest and loneliest things a person can go through in life is heartbreak, especially the first time. It can feel like that pain in the pit of your stomach really might never go away and nothing will ever be okay again. Not only that, but the heightened emotions of heartbreak can spark physiological responses in the body that lead you to feel things physically that are definitely not all in your head. Psychosexual therapist Cate Mackenzie explained in an article for *Stylist* that suffering from a broken heart can send your body into survival mode. To cope with the drastic change and loss our bodies can end up producing an excess of the stress hormone cortisol, which eats away at all the glucose in our system, making us unable to think clearly and manage our daily lives. Another extreme response can be descending into a state of shock, which usually has two outcomes: either a hyper state of energy – being 'adrenalised and unable to switch off' – or an extremely low-energy and dissociative state, both of which are difficult to grasp. So just know that when you really can't think straight or form a complete sentence, you're not just being dramatic – your body is going through it.

DID YOU KNOW?

There's such a thing as Broken Heart Syndrome. In medical terms it's known as stress cardiomyopathy. According to global health enterprise Johns Hopkins Medicine, it's a condition that occurs when 'intense emotional or physical stress can cause rapid and severe heart muscle weakness (myopathy)'. Of course, it's an extreme example that is very rare, but it can occur in cases of grief, fear, anger or surprise.

In other words, your heart is both a figurative and physical object and, as such, it's extremely precious. Taking care of it, protecting it and letting it heal are some of the most important things you can do with it when it's hurting, and Lizzo is a pretty good guide on how to do so.

LIZZO'S HEARTBREAK ANTHEM

For *Billboard*'s 'How It Went Down' series, Lizzo told the story of the making of her first number-one single, 'Truth Hurts', and in case you couldn't tell from the general vibe of the track, it was inspired by heartbreak.

'I didn't want to go to the studio, I was so upset and depressed and sad,' she explains, setting the scene. She'd just received a voicemail from a guy she was seeing and really cared about, basically telling her it's over: 'Don't call me anymore, don't hit me up. I'm getting back with my ex.' Lizzo took the hit and accepted it, blocked him on everything and didn't get back in contact.

Back in the studio, Lizzo opens up to her long-time collaborator, Ricky Reed, about how she's feeling. She explains that she wishes she could have spoken to the guy one more time because if she could have planned it, she would have said, 'Good luck with the person who's supposed to hold you down but holds you back.'

As Lizzo continues to talk, Ricky scribbles down snippets of what she has been saying in a notepad. At the end of the conversation, he shows Lizzo the notes he's been taking and says, 'I hope you know you just wrote a song.'

Ricky lays down a beat, Lizzo goes in to record her vocals and turns her emotional rant into beautiful, powerful music. At the end of the music video for 'Truth Hurts',

Lizzo shouts out, half-jokingly: 'That's how hit records are made! They're made from the heart. They're made from tears, they're made from fears, and they're made from happy endings.'

Lizzo is living proof that there's so much healing to be found in your ability to put words to the feelings that overwhelm you when you're in the depths of heartbreak. In being able to vent your frustrations instead of bottling them up, and then turning them into something great. There really is a silver lining – or a platinum one in this case – to every dark cloud.

If you're experiencing heartbreak at the moment, or know somebody who is, take the time to talk through the pain. The worst thing you can do is brush it under the carpet and bury it. Start by using the space below to write down how the heartbreak makes you feel, and the words you wish you could say to the person who caused it. Nobody needs to see or read this, so be as honest as possible. If anything, as time passes and your heart heals, having your own words to reflect on can prove to be a really helpful and interesting resource for growth.

'Truth Hurts' was originally released in 2017 as a standalone single, but it wasn't until 2019 that the song received a second lease of life when it was featured in Netflix's break-up romcom *Someone Great*, and this heightened visibility inspired an onslaught of usage across TikTok, eventually making the song go viral in all senses of the word. The tune soundtracked the moment when a girl comforts her friend, who's broken up with her boyfriend of nine years. The writer and director of the film, Jennifer Kaytin Robinson, told *Rolling Stone* magazine of the scene,

'It was always my intention for this moment to be able to live outside the film as a stand-alone clip.' And that's exactly what it did. The two buddies sing along loudly in the kitchen to make themselves feel better, and that's the spirit of the song in a snapshot. It's a way of connecting with others through pain and coming through that tunnel to a place of joy, reclaiming that lost sense of power. As a result, the song connected with a whole new audience and climbed up the iTunes and Shazam charts, coinciding perfectly with the track's viral trends on TikTok. The rest is history. The single reached Number One in the *Billboard* charts, making Lizzo the third woman rapper in history to do so without a featured artist, and spent seven weeks there. The track later won her a Grammy for Best Pop Solo Performance and is, at time of writing, certified five-times platinum.

———▷ ....

....

....

....

....

....

....

....

....

LIZZO'S LESSONS IN HEARTBREAK

GET IT ALL OUT

Whatever you're feeling and however you like to express those feelings, the first tip is to make sure you have an outlet. Whether it's a song, a poem, a journal entry or a stream-of-consciousness rant in your Notes app, it's always better out than in. Finding ways to put into words what's happening will really aid the process of understanding the events that have occurred, grasping how you feel about them and identifying the best possible route forward. Plus, who knows? Maybe you'll stumble on your very own 'Truth Hurts'.

SIT IN YOUR FEELINGS

A lot of the time, we have a natural reflex to push negative feelings aside. Catchphrases like 'good vibes only' and 'always look on the bright side' emblazoned on Pinterest give us the impression that negative emotions aren't welcome or necessary if you want to thrive and be happy. That's simply not true. In fact, it's precisely by giving yourself permission to be angry or sad or even numb that you will be able to heal and move on through life in a happy and healthy manner. Lizzo is a huge advocate of talking about feelings, of not being ashamed to cry and of allowing yourself to crumble a little before building yourself back up. Your feelings are always valid and you should never feel guilty for needing time and space to sit in them fully. Surround yourself with people who also know and appreciate the importance of that. Put that soppy film on and cry your eyes out if you need to, curl up in bed and rest or order that takeaway you're craving. Everything else will still be there tomorrow.

BE YOUR OWN SOULMATE
As Lizzo declares in the aptly named 'Soulmate', one of the key benefits of being single is having the space to learn independence. It might not feel like it right now, but this is the best opportunity you could have to take some time to learn about yourself outside of how you are with a partner. Relish the chance to do things just for you, take that solo trip, put whatever you want on the TV or check out that exhibition you've been meaning to go to. This is the time to figure out who you are and what you like, to reflect on where you've been in life already and set out where you'd like to go in the future. From film to TV to music, so much is constantly telling us that we haven't lived until we're in love, until we've found the person who completes us, that if we just keep searching we'll find it but we won't be happy till we have, et cetera, et cetera. But I'm here to tell you that you are a whole-ass human being on your own. Be your own soulmate for now.

REMEMBER THE GOOD
A common coping mechanism for dealing with a break-up is to construct a set narrative about what might have caused things to fall apart the way they did. A good guy and a bad guy, black and white. Sometimes that really is the case, but more often than not, there's also a lot of grey area in between – otherwise you wouldn't have been together, right? While you're mourning the loss of this partnership that served you and probably made you happy for however

long, keep in mind that you are allowed to remember the good, too. Maybe not right away if it's too fresh, but at some point. Don't feel like you have to tell yourself the last few weeks or months or years were a horrible mistake. Don't blame yourself for not seeing it sooner. At the very least, every experience in life is a lesson to be learnt. They're what make you who you are.

TRUST IN THE FUTURE

A super-daunting part of breaking up with someone you care for deeply is simply trying to imagine a future without them. You will likely feel impatient to get to a point where that's no longer hard to do, but it's important to find ways to live in the present and to trust in the fact that what is meant for you will be. Find peace in the uncertainty and stay open to all the possibilities for new experiences, opportunities and people that can step into your life at any point. Anxiety sufferers often struggle with worries about the future and endless streams of 'what ifs', which can prevent you from living life to the fullest. One way that Lizzo deals with her own anxieties is through meditation. Taking even ten minutes at the start of your day to centre yourself and quiet your mind before navigating the world can make all the difference to your outlook and stress levels, giving you perspective and grounding.

ROMANTIC LOVE IS JUST ONE KIND OF LOVE

Last on the list, but perhaps the most important of the bunch, is that romantic love is not the only kind of love we experience in life. This is another falsehood that we have the mainstream media to thank for. As a society, we have placed romantic love on a gigantic pedestal as the Ultimate Goal™ in life. There is a value placed on it that often supersedes familial love (with relatives), platonic love (with friends) and also the love of self. From Disney princesses to teen 'chick flicks' to books, magazines and the arts in general, it's a story that has been sold to us since we were old enough to comprehend the outside world: that until we find a soulmate, we are always one step away from our happy ever after – particularly for female and femme-identifying people. Of course it feels like the world is ending when you've broken up with the person who you love and thought you'd be with forever. But in those moments when you feel truly alone in this world, try to take stock of all the other wonderful people in your life who love you just as hard, and maybe shoot one of them a text.

A BEGINNER'S GUIDE TO MEDITATION

☐ Find yourself a quiet spot to sit, away from all distractions and potential disruptions.

☐ Get nice and comfortable, either sitting on a good cushion or chair, or lying down.

☐ To start, close your eyes and try to focus on your breathing to help slow down the thoughts flying around in your head. Breathe in through your nose and out through your mouth.

☐ As you repeat this, allow your thoughts to come into focus and then disappear in your mind. Trying to force yourself to think about nothing will actually have the opposite effect: your thoughts will inevitably start to crowd in and instead of silencing your mind, you will become fixated on this near-impossible aim of achieving a thoughtless mind from the get-go. So relax your mind and allow thoughts to appear; it's completely natural and okay for this to happen. Imagine seeing the words you're thinking written out in the air in front of you. Acknowledge the thought, watch it free of judgement, and then imagine it slowly dissolving into blank space.

☐ Try this for five minutes at a time and build your way up to longer sessions the more you practise. As little as half an hour a day can do wonders for your emotional health.

HOW TO HACK THE HAPPY

So much of our mental wellbeing is connected to external physical factors around us: vitamins, exercise, sunlight, aromas, sounds, nature, friends and family. For many who share their love of Lizzo online, her music can be a source of happiness and serves as a natural mood-booster when needed. But alongside her contributions to banging playlists worldwide, Lizzo has always heavily promoted ways in which we can encourage peace and positivity within our own bodies, too. Speaking often about everything from her daily meditation routine to her plant-based diet or holistic health practices, such as aromatherapy and crystals, to performing healing flute melodies and using mantras in group meditation sessions on her Instagram, Lizzo leads by example in finding ways to hack the happy and live your best possible life.

Our bodies are incredible vessels and so much of what happens in them – when we feel panicky or stressed, when we feel sad and even when we feel happy – is down to simple (and not so simple) chemistry. Learning different ways to hack the system and jumpstart your happy is a great way to help bring yourself out of the funk that you can sometimes feel stuck in when getting over a break-up. We're going to get science-y for a little bit, but it'll be worth it in the end. The happy chemicals released by our body in moments of joy can be split into four. First off is dopamine, informally known as the reward chemical – it's a hormone and neurotransmitter that just makes you feel good and is key to the brain's own reward system. Next up is serotonin, which is mainly a mood stabiliser, keeping you balanced and functioning fairly smoothly, from your appetite and digestion to sleep, cognitive function and memory. People who are dealing with depression often have lower serotonin levels than they should. Third on the list is our good friend oxytocin, also known as the love hormone. It promotes trust, empathy and bonding with others. It's also essential during childbirth and helps parents to bond with their children. Lastly, we have endorphins. These are the natural pain-relievers of the body, which attempt to fix or respond to pain or discomfort. We usually experience a spike in endorphins as a reward for certain activities. So each of these hormones manifests in different situations, but the four of them combined contribute to one's overall level of happiness. Here are a few small things you can do in everyday life to encourage your body to produce more of them, thus naturally regulating and elevating your mood:

DOPAMINE
Start learning a new skill
Flexing your brain muscles (a non-scientific term) can be a really great way to trigger dopamine. Maybe it's logging on to a language app and completing a French lesson, or making a loaf of bread for the first time. Exercising your memory, motor skills or comprehension can spark that sense of achievement that makes your day a little brighter.

Complete a task
We all know the satisfaction we get from crossing something off our to-do list, especially when it's been staring back at us for a while. Take that leap to wash the dishes or buy groceries or just call your parent, sibling or friend and you will feel victorious. Hell, if you don't have a to-do list, try

writing down just one thing you're already planning to do. Once you've done it, cross the item off your list just for fun!

A self-care activity
The joys of a simple face mask, bubble bath or painting your nails cannot be understated. Indulging in even one of these little you moments will help lift your mood before you know it. Bonus point: music is also an easy winner for increasing your dopamine levels, so sticking on your favourite playlist will double the joy.

Celebrate a small win
Did you wash your hair this morning after putting it off for the last few days, or eat a piece of fruit for the first time all week? Pat yourself on the back! Sometimes these tasks can feel insurmountably hard and just getting that far is a real triumph.

SEROTONIN
Meditating
We've already touched on the benefits of meditation, but there is also a wealth of interesting research on the internet exploring the links between meditation, serotonin and the treatment of anxiety disorders. And there are so many different types of meditation to choose from and trial: from mindfulness to transcendental meditation to sound baths or chant-based methods. It can feel intimidating to jump into any of it for the first time or after a long break, but the only way to overcome that is to just bite the bullet and let it get easier with practice, as it always does. After all, what's the worst that could happen?

Exposure to the sun

This is one that we often take for granted – good old vitamin D. Whether it's getting away to a sunnier country if you have the means, sitting directly by the open window while you have your morning cup of tea or asking for that SAD lamp for Christmas so the shorter days don't get you down, getting the sun on your skin is so important. And if that's just not possible, at least try to take vitamin D supplements in the darker months to boost your levels.

Walk in nature

This one's a little harder to do for those of us who live in cities, but it is so effective. Walking around nature and immersing yourself in fresh air and greenery can do wonders for your mood. For the urbanites among us, try searching for local botanical gardens and smaller, quieter parks that you can spend some time in. There's a Japanese practice known as 'forest bathing', which is pretty much just dwelling in the presence of trees – not the three birch trees down your residential street or the patch of grass in the supermarket car park, but being immersed and surrounded by greenery. The global business website Quartz published an article that said the tradition is 'proven to lower heart rate and blood pressure, reduce stress hormone production, boost the immune system, and improve overall feelings of wellbeing'. Besides the insects and temperamental weather, I see no real downsides.

Running/swimming/cycling

This is the one that everyone always recommends, and in your head you're rolling your eyes thinking, yes, the first thing I want to do after crying for three days straight and surviving on a diet made exclusively of Super Noodles and Oreos is go for a run and realise just how unfit I actually am. And that is a totally valid response. When you're in the depths of a low mood, exercise is often the last thing you want to do, and the hardest. But it's a scientific fact that getting out and moving your body, slowly or quickly, in public or in private, is a sure-fire way to reset your brain and alter your mood. And it doesn't have to be a marathon, either; you can ease yourself in. Try starting the day with 25 star jumps in your pyjamas before you get into the shower, or having a little solo dance party in your room before bed, and go from there. Again, like most things in life, the longer you try, the easier it gets. So the good news is, the first day will always be the most difficult.

OXYTOCIN
Play with a pet
This one needs no real explanation. Playing with animals is a thing that makes you happy on a physiological level. If you don't have a pet of your own, use the excuse to go and visit a friend or family member with one. There are also plenty of dog-sitting sites you can sign up for where trusting owners will let you borrow their dog for a day, so check those out in your local area!

Warm physical contact
Being starved of little intimate moments like greeting friends and family can have negative consequences. Holding someone's hand for a moment, giving your flatmate a hug, getting a cuddle from your friend while you watch TV –

these are the things that help tell you and your brain that You. Are. Loved. And it feels awesome. They're also a great way of showing affection, helping you to grow closer to those around you.

Give someone a compliment
Probably the loveliest suggestion of the lot, it's pretty heartwarming that being kind to others is actually proven to have a positive effect on our own hormone balance, too. While I wouldn't suggest handing out buckets of fake compliments as a means of cheating your way to happiness, I would encourage you to be brave and feel confident in speaking up when you think nice things about people but feel too shy to say them out loud. When that girl on the bus has the bag you just bought, tell her you really like it. When your friend does something thoughtful for you without even asking, don't just say thanks, let them know that you value having them in your life and that they are a truly special individual. Take all the chances you can to spread the love and, in return, watch it come right back to you naturally.

ENDORPHINS
Aromatherapy
The environment you're in can have such a massive impact on your mood, and that includes all five senses. When it comes to smells, they mould your experience more than you might think. Reading up briefly on aromatherapy or simply identifying a couple of key smells that you really like is a super-quick and easy way to alter your surroundings and give you an endorphin boost. Whether it's an essential-oils diffuser, room spray or candles, happy smells = a happy

brain. Citrus scents like lemon, orange or grapefruit have been found to have an energising and uplifting effect, floral scents like lavender, rose and jasmine have a more calming nature, while earthy aromas like cedarwood, patchouli and sage have a more balancing, soothing power.

Watch a comedy
An obvious one here, but laughter really can be the best medicine. Forget about the world and put on one of your favourite films or a stand-up special by a comedian you like that will bring guaranteed chuckles.

Laughter exercise
If you don't have time to sit down for a full-length film, there are quick exercises you can learn to do online for five minutes a day that combine yoga breathing techniques and forms of laughter meditation and chants to release endorphins in your brain and boost your mood.

Dark chocolate
Dark chocolate is filled with an amino acid called tryptophan that helps the brain produce both endorphins and serotonin, giving a feeling of comfort. Spicy food can have a similar effect, simulating a euphoria similar to a 'runner's high' in the brain. So if you can locate some molé or chilli chocolate, you're golden!

‘ My job in this world
is communication:
my music, the songs,
the movement, when I do
interviews, when I do
my banter on stage,
I'm just here to
communicate. ’

LIZZO'S

SOCIAL MEDIA ART

This chapter is a hands-on guide to making the most out of social media. If there's one thing – apart from the music – that Lizzo is known for, it's her Instagram. From her twerk-flute videos to striking selfies or candid to-camera videos, her content is guaranteed to explode across the platform within a matter of minutes. I have no doubt that Lizzo's Instagram, followed by Rihanna's, Ariana Grande's, Beyoncé's mum's and Megan Thee Stallion's, will be archived and displayed in a museum in the year 2300. IT'S ART, PEOPLE!

As with any visual platform, apps like Instagram can feel rooted in ideas of luxury, beauty and the aspirational. And while it's great to have #goals to work towards or dream about, we also have to be cautious about yearning for things that are unattainable or unrealistic. If you buy too deeply into the flawless, picture-perfect images sold to us as reality on social media, it's bound to set you up for disappointment and spark damaging feelings of inadequacy. Especially when it's so hard to remind yourself that what you see on Instagram is hardly ever the full story: it's a carefully curated snapshot.

That's what's so great about accounts like Lizzo's, which feels like a more authentic approach to virtual life, showing the ups and the downs, with and without filters. Here are some of the tips, tricks and takeaways on how we can all adapt and adjust our own relationship with social media to help us connect with others, feel good and spread positivity.

HARNESS THE POWER OF SOCIAL MEDIA

Though it sometimes seems like it, social media isn't a popularity contest. Or, at least, it shouldn't be. Instead, when used thoughtfully, it can be such an incredible place to build a sense of community and immerse yourself in images that go against all the things that mainstream advertising and media are telling us, somewhere you can learn new concepts, see new faces and widen your perspective.

When you take away the price of the phone, apps like Instagram, Twitter and Facebook are all free and accessible. And what that does is democratise the structures that determine who gets support and who is allowed to be seen … to an extent. Of course, there are still a whole host of systems in place that mean success on the app as an influencer is rigged against the marginalised and favours the same usual suspects, but for the most part, we have a choice over what we consume and what we give our energy to while inhabiting these online spaces.

In an age when so much of our lives is lived online, consuming an endless stream of content, those choices we make on what we surround ourselves with play a huge part in how we view ourselves and ultimately how we navigate the world. While many of the stories we see are edited, cropped and Photoshopped to display certain narratives of perfection, success, wealth and 'beauty', it becomes even more important to make the conscious choice to engage with a diverse range of voices, bodies and lifestyles. The difference it can make to your everyday is pretty massive.

In her I Weigh interview with Jameela Jamil, Lizzo touched on the power of using social media in that way.

'Instead of using that tool to look at these people who don't look like you – or the haves and the have-nots – use it to find people who do look like you, people that you can relate to so that you can feel seen and feel beautiful.'

FEEL-GOOD INSTAGRAMMERS

In the spirit of diversifying your feed, here are some IG accounts that live by the philosophies of this book and are guaranteed to brighten up your day a little:

WE'RE NOT REALLY STRANGERS
@werenotreallystrangers

An inquisitive IG feed of philosophical questions and existential statements that get to the core of humanity and present thoughts on how to best live in our minds, in love, in friendship and in life. Founded by Koreen Odiney, the brand has extended into the world of merch, card games and interactive social conversation to get to the heart of what it really is to know another person.

PALOMA ELSESSER
@palomija

Born in London, raised in LA and now based in New York City, Paloma Elsesser is a model and muse in the fashion and beauty spheres, who has worked with Pat McGrath, *i-D*, Savage X Fenty and *Vogue* to name but a few. She is plus-size, political and drop-dead gorgeous, and her feed is a combination of scroll-stopping editorial shots, softly lit selfies and thoughtful takes on intersectional feminism and other social-justice issues.

I WEIGH
@i_weigh
Launched by actor and TV personality Jameela Jamil, I Weigh is a platform cultivated for the aim of radical inclusivity. With discussions ranging from mental health to cancel culture to body positivity, there's always something to think about or learn on their page from a whole host of diverse voices and talent.

GAL-DEM
@galdemzine
gal-dem is a London-based online and print publication and collective, founded and run by women and non-binary people of colour. Initially started in 2015 to help address the issues of elitism and erasure within the media industry, the platform has grown exponentially since then and shares innovative angles on pop culture, politics and everything in between.

QUOTES BY CHRISTIE
@quotesbychristie
Self-described 'graphic designer and quote lover', Quotes by Christie's page is a one-stop shop for inspirational content to both save and share. Filled with every colour under the sun, she shares mantras and encouragements that are guaranteed to brighten up your day.

FLORENCE GIVEN
@florencegiven

Feminist illustrator and bestselling author Florence Given uses her platform to empower women to reclaim their power, shed the weight of internalised misogyny and know their worth through art, fashion and lengthy captions. Her debut book *Women Don't Owe You Pretty* unpacks the attitudes and forces that have been at play on women and their bodies for centuries, and puts forward compelling arguments as to why they should all be thrown in the bin.

NAOMI SHIMADA
@naomishimada

Model and writer Naomi Shimada has a feed full of sunshine. Raised with Japanese, Dutch and Canadian heritage around the world in the UK, US and Spain, there's a free-spirited joy that radiates from her and her content. Interestingly, the book she co-wrote called *Mixed Feelings* is a study on how our digital habits and reliance on social media impacts our emotional state and mental health.

HUMANS OF NEW YORK
@humansofny

Started in 2010, Humans of New York is a simple yet striking blog-turned-movement unfurling the stories of everyday people from all walks of life. Each day a portrait is posted alongside a short story of the person in front of the camera and it serves as a reminder of not just the vastness of humanity, but also the depth and texture of it. And that every person on the street has lived a life and has a story to tell.

GURLS TALK
@gurlstalk

Founded by model Adwoa Aboah, the platform is a safe space to discuss mental health. With its range of compassionate infographics, written content and a conversational podcast, this is the account to follow to help destigmatise whatever you might be going through and find a sense of community.

KAI-ISAIAH JAMAL
@kai_isaiah_jamal

Non-binary model, poet and writer Kai-Isaiah is consistently redefining the boundaries of art, fashion and gender on their IG feed. With deeply moving poetry on current affairs, high-fashion editorials and incredible bulldog puppy content, they are well worth a follow.

STEPHANIE YEBOAH
@stephanieyeboah

Influencer and beauty blogger Stephanie Yeboah is the account to follow for all things body positive. As a self-proclaimed 'body image and self-love advocate', her feed is full of colour, inclusivity and exquisite selfie game.

6 Instead of using that tool to look at these people who don't look like you – or the haves and the have-nots – use it to find people who do look like you. 9

MOBILISE THE MASSES

Of course, it isn't all fun and games on Lizzo's own Instagram feed either. She makes sure to use her platform responsibly as a space to help enact and spark conversations, too. In the run-up to the 2020 US election, she used her platform innovatively on a regular basis to encourage a young and disenfranchised demographic to exercise their right to vote, even recreating the historic 'Uncle Sam' photoshoot at one point. During the socio-political instability that occurred after the deaths of George Floyd and Breonna Taylor, she spoke out deliberately and repeatedly to encourage anti-racist action from her multi-million fanbase. More generally, she often preaches on the importance of kindness when engaging with others online and has created a distinctly safe and joyous community of fans with her platform.

2020 was definitely a year that showcased the power and efficiency of social media, at a time when our entire connection with the world was happening through our phones due to coronavirus and quarantines. As a community we relied on social media like never before – to communicate and disseminate information, organise, educate the masses and start to hold powerful bodies to account for the injustices that happened under their supervision. More than ever, people were using their online platforms to enact change and fight for what's right – a mentality that we should adopt long term when it comes to what social media is meant for, beyond money-making and dating. We have to continue to speak up for what we believe in both on- and offline with our friends and family and anyone who will lend an ear, maintaining social media as a vehicle for education and empathetic learning.

'I was the worst communicator, emotionally, when I was younger ... I would stop talking to my family; I would stop talking to my friends. I would go deeper and deeper into that dark place, and the deeper I went, the harder it was to reach out of it.'

LIZZO
ISN'T AFRAID TO CRY

One of Lizzo's best qualities is her vulnerability. Of course she has this almost blinding glow and a truly magnificent laugh, but she's also not afraid to talk about the tough times. And forgive me if it sounds a little cheesy, but sometimes those rainy days are exactly what helps you appreciate the sunshine. I'm sure that's as true for Lizzo as it is for anyone.

While her music inspires positivity and pure joy, it also expresses so much sensitivity to the full spectrum of human emotions. The album opener and title track from her album *Cuz I Love You* opens with her exclaiming unabashedly that she's crying over her love for someone, before a James Bond-esque brass section punctuates the statement, showing that those feelings of sadness and confusion can be as grand and as valid as the happy ones. It is absolutely okay not to be okay. 'Heaven Help Me' is a desperate plea for her love life to change for the better. And 'Crybaby' is a Prince-esque electric funk-filled banger about her right to cry over a man. She even goes so far as to tell him he should keep his apology and consider it an honour that she's upset. That's the kind of energy we could all use more of in our day-to-day life.

LIZZO GETS SAD, TOO

In a *Vogue* video interview, Lizzo touches on a period in her twenties that she calls the 'summer of silence'. In 2008, after dropping out of the University of Houston where she had been studying classical flute on a music scholarship, Lizzo moved to Denver, Colorado, where her mother and brother were, and just ceased to speak. In multiple interviews she has explained that the decision wasn't as zen-like or dramatic

6 You're not supposed to be happy all the time. You're not supposed to know what you're doing all the time. Especially at this age. But not knowing what you're doing has nothing to do with where you're going ... cherish your journey and respect your journey. **9**

as it has been made to seem, but was actually borne out of a deep sadness and embarrassment at her decision to change her life's course. In an interview with *Elle* magazine she said: 'I was the worst communicator, emotionally, when I was younger ... I would stop talking to my family; I would stop talking to my friends. I would go deeper and deeper into that dark place, and the deeper I went, the harder it was to reach out of it.'

And the story is not an uncommon one among those struggling with mental health. In the moment, it can often feel hard to reach out to a friend or family member and talk about what's going on with you. The temptation is to just shut down instead and retreat further into yourself or find ways of distracting yourself from the pain you're feeling, whether that's sleeping the days away or adopting even less-healthy coping strategies. But unfortunately, these are short-term solutions to what can easily become a long-term problem if left unaddressed. And the hardest bit, as Lizzo says, is that the more you retreat, the harder it seems to come back out again.

It's easier said than done, but once you start, it feels so much better to talk. First and foremost, it's a way for you to acknowledge that something is actually wrong. So often when you experience a dark spell it can feel almost imaginary, like you might just be making it up. But you deserve to have your feelings recognised and validated, because they are exactly that: your feelings. Secondly, it lets those around you become aware of what's happening. What we can't ever do is expect those close to us to be able to read our minds. Life would be a lot easier if they could, but unfortunately it doesn't quite work that way. The third benefit of talking to someone (even if it's just one person, sworn to eternal secrecy with an unbreakable pinky promise) is that if it's what you want to do, you can start to get the help you need. Maybe it's as simple as a therapist referral, a lift to the doctor's to get a refill prescription, or a running partner to get you out of the house and active. And the beauty is that a lot of the time, when you reach the other side of the tunnel, you realise that from these experiences, you've learned so much more about yourself and can even grow closer to the people in your life.

ACTIVITY

THOUGHTS LEFT UNSAID
It can be so hard and scary to verbalise how you feel, and even harder to actually communicate those feelings to another person. This is a little section for those daunting moments.

Feel free to scribble down here any thoughts and feelings that you might have inside that you haven't quite been able to put into words. Hopefully, once written down on the page, whatever feelings have been stirring inside you will feel a little less daunting, easier to overcome and maybe even possible to say out loud.

It would be easy to assume that rich and famous superstars like Lizzo have it all figured out. They're beautiful, successful, they probably have everything they've ever wanted, and here we all are, writing, buying and reading books about just how incredible they are. But that isn't necessarily the case. Achieving the things you want in life professionally is only one piece of a very large puzzle, and there's nothing unnatural or wrong about still feeling unhappy or overwhelmed when, to the outside world, you seem to be doing well. In fact, sometimes there's even an added guilt that you feel when you still aren't happy after achieving the things you set out to in life. You don't stop being human when you become well established.

6 I shut down ... I was depressed and sad, but I used it to create the person that I am today. 9

Since she's been enjoying the spotlight, Lizzo has continued to deal with her fair share of struggles. In the spring of 2018, during a jam-packed tour schedule, she reached breaking point. The breakdown led to her making the decision to start therapy. She has talked about that moment in *Rolling Stone* magazine: 'That was really scary ... But being vulnerable with someone I didn't know, then learning how to be vulnerable with people that I do know, gave me the courage to be vulnerable as a vocalist.' And it's true. Making the step to talk to one person – whoever the least daunting option is for you – can have such a huge knock-on effect in how you live your life. Finding a way to verbalise your feelings makes them seem that little bit less

‘ I'm so blessed
that I can turn
my emotions
and my struggles
into self-care
through music. ’

scary, and once you've said it out loud once or twice, what's the harm in three or four times?

For some people that least-daunting option is a therapist, someone who can offer an objective opinion and who is quite literally paid to listen. There's no complicated real-life consequences of you getting everything off your chest within that safe space. For others, therapy might be their idea of a nightmare. They might want to pull aside the closest person to them because they want to feel safe and nurtured with someone they trust. The key is finding what feels right for you, closing your eyes and taking the leap. Imagine what might have happened if Lizzo had never gone to therapy. Never learnt how to be vulnerable with those around her and so always felt too scared to do that in her music. We'd be living in a world without some of the best self-love anthems of the decade. You never know what might be on the other side of your own emotional journey.

BACKLASH AS A TOOL TO GROW

Speaking of journeys, another part of being in the public eye is sometimes facing a backlash to your actions. That's a journey that even Lizzo is familiar with, but she's always determined to learn from it, too. When Jameela Jamil touches on 'cancel culture' during her I Weigh interview, Lizzo explains: 'I use backlash as a tool to help my artistry and help me communicate with people, because that's my job in this world.' She continues: 'I want to listen to people and learn from people. The more I know, the more I can help us.' It's this kind of thoughtfulness and emotional maturity that has allowed Lizzo to evolve and adapt endlessly over the last few years. Instead of being afraid of the tougher times, she has taken them as opportunities to interact and develop. It's a really crucial outlook to have on life as we grow up – that feedback is a necessary tool for growth, instead of a personal insult.

' I didn't want
to be famous,
to be famous,
I wanted to be like
Brandon Boyd
from Incubus! '

LIZZO

MERGES MUSICAL WORLDS

aving grown up in a very musically eclectic household, it's not surprising that throughout the early stages of her career Lizzo played in a number of groups that ranged all the way from hip-hop to prog-rock. Her classical influences began at the age of 12 when she started to learn the flute, and although she was afraid of the jazz and rock iterations of the instrument, playing classically really spoke to her. She grew to love 'the man with the golden flute'. Not the Pied Piper but James Galway, an Irish legend among flute players. In an interview with David Letterman, Lizzo exclaimed, 'He's got a platinum flute. I was like, "What a baller."'

At the same time, young flautist Lizzo was a baller in her own right, too. She described her middle-school band as 'the baddest band in the land' during the Letterman interview and cited it as a signpost in her life of when she really fell in love with music. The band director would transpose songs from the radio and get the students to play along and dance, really putting on a show.

When Lizzo got to college, she excelled at her studies, particularly in the group performance classes where each student would play a piece before getting critiques from the teacher. But when she veered towards a career as a singer/artist, people actually discouraged her from playing the flute at all! 'I had a lot of band-nerd guilt.' In the beginning she didn't defend the decision and instead listened to what she assumed was fair and constructive feedback on what was 'cool'. And so for a long while, flute-playing Lizzo and rap Lizzo parted ways in public.

It wasn't until she trusted in her own instincts and performed with her flute at a live show in Iowa in 2018 before

posting the video on social media that she realised those naysayers had been wrong all along. After that video, the flute took on a life of its own! Within a few minutes, a #fluteandshootchallenge

❛ My music is for everybody ❜

spread like wildfire. It just goes to show that the best possible path you can take is the one that feels most natural and authentic to you. Never mind if it's a path no one has trodden before you; sometimes it pays to be the first if you can just take that step. The relief that comes with no longer pretending to be someone else is something Lizzo knows all about: 'I was so satisfied, because I was known as a flute player now. Secret's out: I am a band nerd.'

Heavily shaped by the gospel sounds of her childhood, Lizzo has continued to incorporate a gospel choir in many of her anthemic hits. The uplifting, spiritual joy that is synonymous with gospel music can be heard on tracks like 'Heaven Help Me' and 'Good as Hell'. The former opens with recognisably slamming church piano chords as Lizzo pleads with the heavens to save her from being destroyed by love. 'Good as Hell' has similarly warm, almost-spiritual elements, but feels like the exultant song that might come after that prayer has been answered, as she returns to form feeling as amazing as the title suggests. Even on her 2016 EP *Coconut Oil*, the track 'Worship' merges the handclap rhythms of energetic gospel choirs and marching-band funk as she soulfully belts for her man to show her his undying love.

It's no surprise that Lizzo's music has such huge crossover appeal, given the breadth of her own tastes and her involvement in a whole catalogue of genre-spanning

DID YOU KNOW?

As a child, Lizzo had dreams of becoming an astronaut. Despite growing up singing in the church choir in Detroit, she was more known for being the brainy one than for her singing ability. But one of her hobbies was writing fantasy stories with strong female characters and eventually that turned into a love of the anime genre. As a kid, she was teased for both her interest in anime and for being a band nerd. Nowadays Lizzo is very vocal about her obsession with the manga series *Sailor Moon* and even dressed up as the lead character on stage at Voodoo Fest in New Orleans.

❝ Keep playing your instrument, man, 'cause people jealous of me 'cause I still play the flute! ❞

groups – from progressive rock band Elypseas to electro-pop duo Lizzo & the Larva Ink – before she catapulted to fame. She helped form the all-girl R&B group The Cornrow Clique when she was still a teenager, inspired by her love of Destiny's Child – the girls would even call in to radio stations and freestyle during the listener segments. Up until 2012, Lizzo was also a part of hip-hop collective GRRRL PRTY, where she flexed her lyrical wit. She was also a member of R&B girl group I.N.I.T.I.A.L.S for a stint! Although The Chalice is arguably the group that gained the most commercial success, Lizzo took a little with her from each of the musical collaborations in her life.

A LIZZO EDUCATION PLAYLIST

If you're inspired by the wealth of influences that go into creating the unique sound of Lizzo and you want to know more, here's a starter playlist to take you on a musical journey of some of the tracks that made her.

'THE RAIN', MISSY ELLIOTT

This iconic bop was the lead single from Missy Elliott's debut album *Supa Dupa Fly*, accompanied by what went on to be one of the most era-defining hip-hop videos of its time, directed by Hype Williams. Lizzo is notably a huge Missy Elliott fan and raves about the rapper-producer-writer every chance she gets. While curating a playlist of songs that soundtracked her life for *Teen Vogue*, she dubbed Elliott 'the only unicorn we've ever had' before adding: 'protect her at all costs'.

'LOSE MY BREATH',
DESTINY'S CHILD

This pick is a special one. *Survivor* was the first album Lizzo ever bought, and when she was in the fifth grade, she skipped school to go and see the group perform at her local Walmart. Lizzo goes on about the significance of this one as a young kid playing in band: 'I thought it was the coolest thing in the world to reappropriate marching bands and make 'em tight because I got made fun of so much for being a band nerd. And then I was like, well, Beyoncé dances to snare drums!' She also makes sure to give a special shoutout to Michelle's verse on the track, which is particularly fire.

'KNUCK IF YOU BUCK',
CRIME MOB

'This song made me wanna be a rapper,' Lizzo says of this tune. It has an unbelievable effect on any audience old enough to remember its significance when it dropped in 2004 – from friendly moshes to old-school dance moves, it's bound to get a crowd moving. 'I just remember feeling so black and so cool and so trill,' is what Lizzo recalls of the first time she heard it.

6 I used to be so
upset that I never
had co-signs.
I was like, "I'm too
weird for the rappers
and too black for the
indies." I was just
sitting in this
league of my own. **9**

'GOODIES',
CIARA

During a video for *Teen Vogue*, Lizzo reminisces about borrowing her dad's convertible and driving around with her friends blaring this out loud and proud. The track was actually the debut single from Ciara, and what a statement of intent it was. From the intricate choreography to the extremely Noughties' wardrobe and celeb cameos, it's a visual track that is definitely solid in the memories of an entire generation of kids who grew up watching music-video channels.

'PARTY',
BEYONCÉ FROM *HOMECOMING:*
THE LIVE ALBUM

Taken from the live recorded album of Beyoncé's seminal Coachella performance, this track really showcases some of the infectious marching-band spirit that helped make Lizzo the character she is today. And with her also being a fully-fledged member of the Beyhive, it only made sense to include another track by the fellow Houston native. The original version of 'Party' also features a stellar verse from Outkast rapper André 3000, who also contributed hugely to the Southern rap scene during his time in the group.

'WAX SIMULACRA', THE MARS VOLTA

Dubbed by Lizzo as 'one of the hardest prog-rock songs', this tune by The Mars Volta is not for the faint-hearted. But with drum solos that make you a little dizzy and a strangely hypnotic falsetto topline, it takes you on a real journey. 'The lead singer of The Mars Volta was my inspiration. I wanted to sing and go crazy like him on stage.'

'THEME FROM *JURASSIC PARK*', JOHN WILLIAMS

John Williams, who Lizzo describes as 'the greatest American composer', is responsible for so many of the great melodies from the movies, from the suspense-filled two-note *Jaws* soundtrack to the iconic themes from *E.T.*, *Indiana Jones*, *Superman*, the first three *Harry Potter* films and the original *Star Wars* trilogy. In the *Jurassic Park* theme he excelled, too, of course, creating a composition as full of awe and beauty as the dinosaurs it was made to soundtrack. Lizzo remembers, 'The first time I heard *Jurassic Park*, I didn't quite understand getting goosebumps with a movie score, but I just remember humming that … it's just lit!'

'WARM WINDS', SZA

'Warm Winds' is what some might call an SZA deep cut. From her mixtape EP Z and featuring TDE labelmate Isaiah Rashad, the track pre-dates her biggest work, debut album *Ctrl*. For Lizzo, SZA is 'one of my favourite R&B writers of this time ... this song really did something to me because it's really weird and it sounds like The Beatles. I love the way that she thinks and I love how that comes out in music.' The two women have toured together and most recently during lockdown met up on Instagram Live to co-host a sound bath and flute meditation session. Lizzo finishes her rave review of the singer by adding hastily, 'If you don't appreciate her at her "Warm Winds", you don't deserve her at her "Love Galore" and that's that.'

'THE GREY HAVENS', HOWARD SHORE FEAT. SIR JAMES GALWAY

This final choice might seem a little rogue upon first listen, but stay with me. Yes, it's from the soundtrack album for the third film in the *Lord of the Rings* trilogy, *The Return of the King*. But it features Lizzo's very own favourite flute player, Sir James Galway. Composed by Howard Shore, the piece has a typically *LOTR* sound – soothing, but somehow still completely epic. *Pro tip: Soundtracks like* The Lord of the Rings *are amazing to work or revise to when you really need to get your head down – complex enough to not be repetitive; interesting enough that you don't get bored; muted enough without the vocals that you don't get distracted.*

6 I was like, "I'm afraid of my voice. I'm afraid of people thinking that I'm one thing." I had to just lose that fear, because the more people get to know me, the more they'll realize I have many, many, many levels to me. **9**

'Work hard, play hard and do it 'cause you love it.'

LIZZO

KNOWS HOW TO HAVE FUN

From the meme references and jokes littered throughout, to the catchy hooks made to be sung in cars with friends and at parties, you can't help but have fun with Lizzo's music!

Songs like 'Juice' are so joyous and completely contagious. As soon as you hear it, it's impossible to do anything other than sing along and feel good while you're doing it. And none of that was an accident. Lizzo, her producer Ricky Reed and her songwriter Theron Thomas broke down the process of writing hit single 'Juice' for the *New York Times*'s 'Diary of a Song' series. When they were in the studio the day they made 'Juice', Lizzo actually said to her producer, 'Ricky, I want you to play a song that is a f***ing undeniable hit.' And the instrumental for 'Juice' was what he chose. Theron Thomas remembers hearing it for the first time and says, 'It made me want to dance, it made me feel like, yo, this has a throwback feel, but they definitely made it in 2019.' The lyrics in the first line of the track came to him naturally, while Reed admits that, 'Sometimes when I'm in a session and an artist sings one line, I can't help but jump on the talk-back and be like, "This is gonna be crazy!"'

When it came to the call-and-response bridge of the song, they initially had a line about not having to try because you wake up looking good, but Lizzo pushed back: 'It's not just about waking up pretty, what do we really mean underneath that? I was born like this. That means I love me for me, no matter what make-up I have on, what weave I have on, whether I got my lash extensions on or not.' The word 'juice' was picked to capture the playful essence of the song in one word: 'I think juice is kind of freaky,' says Lizzo, 'it's kind of spiritual and special.' From the get-go Thomas

FUN FACT

The back-up vocals that form the call-and-response part of the bridge in 'Juice' are not professional vocalists. In the studio, Thomas had the idea of getting some group vocals into the track to help bolster Lizzo's lyrics and create a kind of girl-gang vibe. Lizzo responded with the suggestion that instead of hiring strangers, she could bring her friends in to record the layers. Thomas recalls that 'three or four of her best friends came down to the studio and they were just like … lit!' So on the final version of Lizzo's single, the voices you hear on the song are Lizzo's actual besties. Aww! It's lovely to think that the fun we all have while listening to the song is in some small way inspired by the genuine fun and friendship that was had while making the music in the studio. Lizzo says, 'It's the little details like that [which] make something [go] from a good song to a magical moment.'

said, 'Whatever it is that we do, I want people to hear and I want people to smile.' Reed feels that way now, saying, 'It honestly just feels so, so super joyful listening to it back.'

LIZZO BREAKS THE INTERNET

Alongside Lizzo's music, one of the most joyous reflections of her spirit is her live shows, which provide the opportunity for fans to bask in her energy IRL. From her band to the extravagant outfits, the choreography, the twerking, the flute-playing and the backing dancers, it's just a festival for the soul. But for one woman in particular, Lizzo made a show into a night she'll never forget. Professor of Gender and Women's Studies at the University of Wisconsin–Madison Dr Sami Schalk is a huge fan of Lizzo, and began tweeting #twerkwithlizzo in an attempt to grab the star's attention and hopefully an invite to dance with her on stage at one of her live shows. For over a week Dr Schalk tweeted the hashtag, discussing best outfit options and eventually posting a video of herself in a homemade glitter cape with '100% THAT B*TCH' plastered across it. The video gained over 45,000 views in a day with the caption: 'Final attempt at getting @lizzo's attention for her show tomorrow in #MadisonWI at @TheSylvee with this cape I made. All I wanna do is #twerkwithlizzo. Retweet to make this fat black queer bitch's dreams come true.'

After turning up to the show hours early to secure a front-row spot and holding the cape up for her to see, the professor was brought up on stage by Lizzo's team and her dream came true: they twerked together. The subsequent video of the night also went viral and invited a whole host of love and support, as well as a fair few trolls. But ultimately, it was a truly liberating and I'm sure life-changing experience for Dr Schalk and is a testament to the power of spreading joy. In living your best life visibly and unabashedly, you give others the courage to do the same, creating a snowball effect.

In a piece that the professor wrote about that night, she unpacks the concept of 'pleasure activism', a concept coined by activist, writer and theorist adrienne maree brown. It's the idea that 'we all need and deserve pleasure, and that our social structures must reflect this. In this moment, we must prioritise the pleasure of those most impacted by oppression.' In having fun and taking moments to laugh, dance and heal, we use joy as an act of resistance.

LIZZO DOES MEME CULTURE

Another way that Lizzo sparks joy for others is through her unmatched sense of humour, twinned with her knowledge of meme culture. One of the best examples of this was when she recreated the hilarious scene from *Anchorman* in which Will Ferrell's character Ron Burgundy launches into a surreal jazz flute performance on a night out. With Lizzo starring in Ferrell's place, she climbs over tables while performing a flute rendition of 'Juice', spitting fire from the end of the instrument and even popping up under someone's cubicle in the toilets.

The idea came from a video she posted on Instagram of her practising her jazz flute, in which she made the joke, 'Somebody tell Will Ferrell I wanna battle him,' in reference to the movie. She told Radio Free KJLH during an interview: 'And then a few months later Will Ferrell dresses up as Ron Burgundy and he's like, "Lizzo, I accept your challenge," and then he pulls his flute out and starts going. I was like, wait a second! So I gotta up the ante.' It's a truly hilarious way to spend two and a half minutes of your day.

STANDOMS UNITE

In addition to all of the politics and activism and discourse that surrounds Lizzo, the core of her message is one of enjoyment, and that's part of the reason it spreads so far. She even found a fan in Harry Styles after he covered 'Juice' for Radio 1's Live Lounge. Two months later she brought him out on stage for her SiriusXM performance in Miami and the pair looked like they might be having more fun than the crowd, holding hands and even doing a little planned choreography together. After that, the love fest continued when Lizzo landed in the UK and performed his single 'Adore You' for her Radio 1 Live Lounge performance, even joking during her fan Q&A that her 'favourite British import would be Harry Styles'. When the two were sat near each other at the BRIT Awards not long afterwards they shared an adorable moment as Styles rested his head softly on her shoulder and, honestly, the kinetic energy of Harry Styles's stanbase multiplied by the hardcore Lizzbians, all vibrating with glee at the union, is probably enough to power all the outlets in New York City for a year. We may have just found the newest sustainable power source.

‘ There's power
in who you are,
there's power in
your voice. ’

LIZZO

DNA TEST

THAT B**** DNA TEST

Answer the following questions to discover exactly what percentage 'that b*tch' you are ...

How would your best friend describe you in one word?
a. Lovely
b. Wildcard
c. Goddess

When you're relaxing after a long day, you go to put on ...
a. *Survivor* by Destiny's Child
b. *Ctrl* by SZA
c. *Cuz I Love You* by Lizzo

You're going on a first date. What's the outfit vibe?
a. Subtle, calm and collected
b. Crazy, sexy, cool
c. Whatever vibe I feel like in the moment

Someone comes for you on Twitter. What do you do?
a. Deactivate your account – you don't need that stress
b. Come back with the same energy
c. It depends what they're saying – can I have more details?

What do you look for in a partner?
a. Someone who treats me like a queen
b. Someone who can handle me
c. Someone who makes me a better person

Go-to Netflix-and-chill series?

a. *Parks and Rec*

b. *Insecure*

c. *Girlfriends*

Who would be your celebrity best friend?

a. Harry Styles

b. Beyoncé

c. My real friends are more than enough!

One thing you'd change in the world if you could?

a. I'd make everyone nicer

b. No men in positions of power

c. Solve world hunger

What's your favourite brand?

a. Nike

b. Gucci

c. Telfar

What does your dream home look like?

a. An adorable cottage in the woodlands

b. A loft-style apartment with a view

c. An old but renovated three-storey house with a garden and a cinema room

MOSTLY AS: 70–79 PER CENT 'THAT B*TCH'

Just based on the fact that you either bought or were given this book, are reading it and have made it this far, there's no doubt that you're already aceing the 'Being That B*tch' test. So congratulations for that. You've got great taste in music, you're a joy to be around, but maybe you haven't quite figured out the best way to come out of your shell yet. Sometimes you might doubt yourself or try to tone down your shine when you're feeling the pressure. Don't panic or force anything, though; you're already on the right path. That confidence will come with time if you want it to. Keep doing what you're doing and trust in your instincts. The rest will follow naturally.

MOSTLY BS: 80–89 PER CENT 'THAT B*TCH'

You are so close to achieving true 100-per-cent 'that b*tch' status. You've got the fire, you speak your mind and you radiate positivity to anyone who comes across you. If anything, at times you may struggle with being a little bit volatile and letting your emotions get the better of you. So be sure to have a go at some of those quick and easy meditation and laughter exercises in Chapter 3 (see page 67) when you need to find a little calm in your mind. Once you nail that balance, there'll be nothing stopping you.

MOSTLY CS: 90–100 PER CENT 'THAT B*TCH'

Wow. Look at us. Who'd have thought. You. Are. That. B*tch. Don't let anyone tell you otherwise. You brighten up everyone's day who has the pleasure of meeting you, you champion the underdogs in any way you can and, most importantly, you are your most authentic self. Sometimes that means having a cry and a moment of quiet, and sometimes it's shouting from the rooftops. The best thing about being 'that b*tch' is that there really is not much advice left to give you, because you know in your heart of hearts that it doesn't really matter what anyone else thinks, as long as you're secure in yourself! Ten out of ten. Well done, you.

WHICH LIZZO SONG ARE YOU?

1. Ideal date scenario
a. Amusement park (1)
b. Coffee and croissants (3)
c. Dinner and a movie (2)

2. If you could have any pet, you'd want ...
a. A puppy (2)
b. A kitten (3)
c. An iguana (1)

3. Best way to spend a weekend?
a. Netflix and chill (2)
b. Out on the town (1)
c. Solo cinema trip (3)

4. What's your favourite app?
a. Twitter (3)
b. Instagram (2)
c. TikTok (1)

5. Pick a vacation spot
a. New York City (1)
b. The Bahamas (3)
c. The Swiss Alps (2)

6. Your favourite way to get around?
a. Uber (2)
b. Train (1)
c. Walking all the way (3)

7. If you could only wear one piece of jewellery …
a. Necklace (3)
b. Earrings (1)
c. Rings galore (2)

8. Best meal of the day?
a. Breakfast (3)
b. Lunch (2)
c. Dinner (1)

9. What keeps you company in the car?
a. Bespoke playlist (2)
b. Podcasts (3)
c. Radio (1)

10. Would you rather …?
a. Twerk (3)
b. Play the flute (2)
c. Rap (1)

'TRUTH HURTS': 0–10

You're resilient and full of fire. Sometimes things don't go your way, but you bounce back better than before. Those trials and tribulations that feel hard to overcome now will soon be a thing of the past. Until you find someone who can love you for all that you are, you'll do just fine on your own, thank you very much!

'JUICE': 10–20

You're an unstoppable force and no one would dare tell you otherwise. You believe in yourself so wholeheartedly that it doesn't even matter what other people think: just the way it should be. You're lovable, funny and a joy to be around. Spending time with those you're close to feeds your soul for the better, so keep doing it.

'GOOD AS HELL': 20–30

You are thriving and it shows. You've got your head screwed on properly and the glowing energy inside you radiates to everyone you come across. When you walk into a room all eyes are on you and you know it, but you don't act up for attention either.

HOW WELL DO YOU KNOW LIZZO?

1. In what year was Lizzo born?
a. 1990
b. 1988
c. 1980
d. 1985

2. Where was she born?
a. Houston, Texas
b. Denver, Colorado
c. Detroit, Michigan
d. Minneapolis, Minnesota

3. What's her real first name?
a. Melissa
b. Elizabeth
c. Eliza
d. Lisa

4. What critically acclaimed 2019 film did she have a cameo in?
a. *Someone Great*
b. *Always Be My Maybe*
c. *Hustlers*
d. *Captain Marvel*

5. Which celebrity covered her hit single 'Juice' on BBC Radio 1 Live Lounge, as well as while touring?

a. Ariana Grande

b. Charli XCX

c. Harry Styles

d. Niall Horan

6. Which comedian did she twerk on during a late-night TV performance?

a. Jack Whitehall

b. Chris Rock

c. Romesh Ranganathan

d. Amy Schumer

7. Which singer did Lizzo host a sound bath and flute meditation session with live on Instagram?

a. Kehlani

b. SZA

c. Solange

d. Janelle Monáe

8. Which Lizzo song did not get nominated for a Grammy at the 2020 ceremony?

a. 'Truth Hurts'

b. 'Jerome'

c. 'Exactly How I Feel'

d. 'Juice'

9. What category did Lizzo not win a Grammy for at the same ceremony?

a. Urban Contemporary

b. Pop

c. Gospel

d. R&B

10. How many times has Lizzo's first number-one single 'Truth Hurts' gone platinum?

a. 1

b. 9

c. 3

d. 5

11. Which rapper helped inspire Lizzo's stage name?

a. Kanye West

b. Missy Elliott

c. Jay-Z

d. P. Diddy

12. Which social media platform was directly responsible for the delayed commercial success of her hit single 'Truth Hurts'?

a. Instagram

b. TikTok

c. Twitter

d. Musical.ly

13. Which TV celebrities collaborated with Lizzo on the campaign for album single 'Soulmate'?
a. RuPaul
b. Chrissy Teigen
c. Jameela Jamil
d. The cast of *Queer Eye*

14. What is the name of Lizzo's beloved flute?
a. Sasha
b. Sarah
c. Stella
d. Natasha

15. Which of these is not a concept from one of Lizzo's videos?
a. 1980s fitness
b. Wedding
c. Synchronised swimming
d. At the hairdresser's

A SONG FOR EVERY OCCASION

IT'S GOING TO BE A GOOD DAY ...
'JUICE'
Encapsulating the Lizzo spirit in one fell swoop, 'Juice' is a song about believing in your sauce and being proud of it. Made in the studio with two of her long-time collaborators and a group of her best girlfriends, this song signals fun times to be had. It'll pump you up and get you feeling ready to conquer anything and everything.

WHEN YOU CAN DO BETTER ...
'JEROME'
This track is for when you've had enough of someone taking you for granted. Even though you care for them deeply and it's hard to imagine a life without them, sometimes there's nothing left to do but call it quits. In those moments, blast this out loud and sing along at full lung capacity. Then shake it off – tomorrow's a new day and something better is guaranteed to be right around the corner.

AFTER A BREAK-UP ...
'SOULMATE'
'Soulmate' is a track that could send you either way after a break-up, making you laugh or cry. Whichever happens is the right response. A song like this is best enjoyed when taking a moment in brand-new pyjamas or a lavender bubble bath, with the speaker on extra loud. It celebrates the power of knowing one thing for

certain: that at least you will always be there for you. And let me tell you, sometimes that's all that matters.

WHEN YOU'RE A LITTLE TOO LOVESTRUCK ... 'HEAVEN HELP ME'

This is a song to snap you out of it. You know that kind of love that you fall into a little too hard or a little too deep because what's the worst that could happen? The one that makes you forget to call your mum back or text your bestie? 'Heaven Help Me' is a call to the heavens, asking them to put an end to that kind of unhealthy obsession. For everyone's sake.

TO PUMP YOU UP FOR THE GYM ... 'LIKE A GIRL'

Whenever you're lacking a bit of pizzazz, this tune is a sure-fire cure. With a catchy, gender-subverting chorus and a perfect tempo to squat to, 'Like a Girl' is the song to arm your gym playlist with for that final push on the treadmill and to remind you that you can do literally anything you put your mind to in life.

WHEN YOU'RE FEELING HURT ... 'CRYBABY'

Equal parts sad and theatrical, this Prince-like hazy number is inspired by those moments of weakness, when you just need to let it all out. Lizzo is letting you know that there's absolutely nothing wrong with that – sometimes you just gotta relinquish control and wallow in it. We go again tomorrow.

WHEN YOU'RE FEELING HUNGRY ...
'BATCHES & COOKIES'

A fairly self-explanatory one here, this is a sickly-sweet banger from the early days of Lizzo: a perfect snacking anthem. It features some really vibrant food imagery throughout the track that really gets the stomach rumbling ...

WHEN YOUR LOVE IS UNREQUITED ...
'GOOD AS HELL'

This song tells you you're better than this. No more moping around. Onto the next. There's no pain quite like unrequited love, and yet there's also nothing more futile than stressing over the things in life you can't change. It's a real catch-22 ... While you attempt to figure out whether the person you're fawning over is really worth all the tears, plug in, put this on and buy that new jumper you've been eyeing up.

PARTING WISDOM

TAKE A RISK AND BET ON YOUR DREAMS. The worst thing that can happen is you tried …

LOVE YOUR BODY WITH EVERYTHING YOU'VE GOT. Not because someone else tells you that it's beautiful, but because you truly believe it for yourself.

DON'T BE AFRAID TO CRY IT OUT. We all need to sometimes. Even Lizzo.

SPEAK YOUR MIND and speak up for your community.

LEARN TO HACK THE HAPPY IN LIFE. Surround yourself with good people, reclaim joy in the small things and treat yourself how you'd like to be treated by others.

RELISH THE QUIET MOMENTS. Sometimes they're even more revolutionary than the loud ones.

LISTEN AND TALK IN EQUAL MEASURE. Sometimes the best thing you can do for someone else is just be there.

HARNESS THE POWER OF SOCIAL MEDIA to reflect the world we actually live in, to exchange knowledge and find your community.

RESOURCES

INTRODUCTION: INSPIRED BY LIZZO

Spanos, Brittany, 'The Joy of Lizzo', *Rolling Stone*, 22 January 2020

1. LIZZO'S LESSONS IN SELF-CONFIDENCE

Lizzo, TikTok, 9 June 2020

'Lizzo: The Truth About Self-acceptance', StyleLikeU, 20 October 2014

My Next Guest ... with David Letterman with Lizzo, Netflix, 21 October 2020

Rampton, John, 'The Benefits of Playing Music Help Your Brain More Than Any Other Activity', Inc.com, 21 August 2017

'Extended Video: Lizzo', CBS Sunday Morning, 6 October 2019

'Lizzo Collaborated with Prince for His 2014 Album Plectrumelectrum', PopBuzz.com

Spanos, Brittany, 'The Joy of Lizzo', *Rolling Stone*, 22 January 2020

'Lizzo Shares Her F-ckboy Stories, Talks Self-love, Confidence, New Music + More', Breakfast Club Power 105.1FM, 24 May 2019

'Lizzo x Jameela Jamil on Finding Confidence & Dealing w/ Social Media Criticism', I Weigh/Jameela Jamil, 12 September 2020

'73 Questions with Lizzo', Vogue. com, 24 September 2020

'Lizzo: My First ... Lizzo on Her First Crush, First Kiss, and First Concert', Vogue.co.uk, 7 November 2019

Rankine, Claudia, 'Lizzo on Hope, Justice, and the Election', Vogue. com, 24 September 2020

Takeda, Allison, 'What the World Needs Now Is More Lizzo', Elle. com, 5 September 2019

Kennedy, Gerrick D., '100% Her Year: How Lizzo Became the One Thing We All Loved in 2019', *Los Angeles Times*, 11 December 2019

2. LIZZO SAYS LOVE YOUR BODY

Lizzo, TikTok, 9 June 2020

'Lizzo on the Power of Words', CBS News, 28 June 2020

My Next Guest ... with David Letterman with Lizzo, Netflix, 21 October 2020

'73 Questions with Lizzo', Vogue.com, 24 September 2020

Esmonde, Katelyn, 'What Jillian Michaels Got Wrong About Lizzo and Body Positivity', Vox.com, 15 January 2020

Spanos, Brittany, 'The Joy of Lizzo', *Rolling Stone*, 22 January 2020

'Lizzo: Tiny Desk Concert', NPR.org, 5 August 2019

'Lizzo On Her First Crush, First Kiss, and First Concert', Vogue.co.uk, 7 November 2019

Lopez, Julyssa, '"Truth Hurts" Was a Viral Hit, But Lizzo's Stardom Is No Accident', Billboard.com, 19 September 2019

Yeboah, Stephanie, 'Body Positivity: Why the Work Is Far from Finished', Vogue.co.uk, 30 May 2020

Rankine, Claudia, 'Lizzo on Hope, Justice, and the Election', Vogue.com, 24 September 2020

'Lizzo x Jameela Jamil on Finding Confidence & Dealing w/ Social Media Criticism', I Weigh/Jameela Jamil, 12 September 2020

3. LIZZO'S GUIDE TO HEARTBREAK

Wynn, Aiden, 'Heartbreak: This Is What Happens to Our Bodies During a Break-up', Stylist.co.uk, undated

'Broken Heart Syndrome', *Hopkins Medicine*, undated

'How Lizzo Created "Truth Hurts" | Billboard | How It Went Down', Billboard YouTube channel, 24 September 2019

Spanos, Brittany, 'The Joy of Lizzo', *Rolling Stone*, 22 January 2020

Raypole, Crystal, 'Happy Hormones: What They Are and How to Boost Them', Healthline.com, 30 September 2019

Livni, Ephrat, 'The Japanese Practice of "Forest Bathing" Is Scientifically Proven to Improve Your Health', Quartz (qz.com), 12 October 2016

Sharma, Uma and Pagano, Alyssa,
'What Happens to Your Brain
and Body When You Eat a Hot
Pepper', BusinessInsider.com, 12
October 2017

4. SOCIAL MEDIA IN THE AGE OF LIZZO

'Lizzo x Jameela Jamil on Finding
Confidence & Dealing w/ Social
Media Criticism', I Weigh/Jameela
Jamil, 12 September 2020

5. LIZZO ISN'T AFRAID TO CRY

Takeda, Allison, 'What the World
Needs Now Is More Lizzo', Elle.
com, 5 September 2019

'Lizzo on the Power of Words', CBS
News, 28 June 2020

'73 Questions with Lizzo', Vogue.
com, 24 September 2020

Spanos, Brittany, 'The Joy of Lizzo',
Rolling Stone, 22 January 2020

'Lizzo x Jameela Jamil on Finding
Confidence & Dealing w/ Social
Media Criticism', I Weigh/Jameela
Jamil, 12 September 2020

6. LIZZO MERGES MUSICAL WORLDS

Irby, Samantha, 'Lizzo: TIME's
Entertainer of the Year', TIME,
2019

My Next Guest ... with David
Letterman with Lizzo, Netflix, 21
October 2020

'Lizzo on the Power of Words', CBS
News, 28 June 2020

Spanos, Brittany, 'The Joy of Lizzo',
Rolling Stone, 22 January 2020

Spanos, Brittany, 'How Lizzo
Conquered Her Fears and Found
Her Best Self', Rolling Stone, 19
April 2019

Alexander, Ella, 'Introducing Lizzo:
The Flute-playing Rapper Who
Has a Lot to Say on Ferguson',
The Independent, 26 August
2014

'Lizzo Creates the Playlist of Her
Life', Teen Vogue, 15 June 2018

'Lizzo Shares Her F-ckboy Stories,
Talks Self-love, Confidence, New
Music + More', Breakfast Club
Power 105.1FM, 24 May 2019
Spanos, Brittany, 'The Joy of Lizzo',
Rolling Stone, 22 January 2020

143

7. LIZZO KNOWS HOW TO HAVE FUN

'73 Questions with Lizzo', Vogue. com, 24 September 2020

'How Lizzo Made "Juice" as Joyous as She Is | Diary of a Song', *New York Times*, 23 April 2019

Schalk, Sami, 'When I Twerked Onstage with Lizzo, It Was an Act of Political Defiance', Vox. com, 18 October 2019

'Lizzo Discusses Appearing on *The Daily Show*, Playing the Flute and Recreating Will Ferrell Scene', RadioFreeTV, 16 April 2019

'Harry Styles – "Juice" (Lizzo Cover) in the Live Lounge', BBC Radio 1, 18 December 2019

'Lizzo – "Adore You" (Harry Styles Cover) in the Live Lounge', BBC Radio 1, 17 February 2020

Aniftos, Rania, 'Here's Every Time Lizzo & Harry Styles Showed Each Other Love', Billboard. com, 18 February 2020

8. DNA TEST

'Lizzo's Inspiring BBMAs Speech: 'There's Power In Who You Are', Access YouTube channel, 15 October 2020